THE LAST CONFESSION

Roger Crane

THE LAST CONFESSION

OBERON BOOKS
LONDON

Characters

CARDINAL GIOVANNI BENELLI

At the time of his confession, he is the Cardinal of Florence. When the action of the play begins, five years earlier, he is an Archbishop holding the number two position in the office of the Secretary of State in the Vatican. Because of his close relationship with Pope Paul VI, he is the second most powerful figure in the Church.

THE CONFESSOR

A priest, approximately sixty years old. He has come to hear Cardinal Benelli's confession.

CARDINAL ALBINO LUCIANI

The Cardinal of Venice. He becomes Pope John Paul I.

CARDINAL JEAN VILLOT

The Secretary of State of the Vatican.

BISHOP PAUL MARCINKUS

The highest ranking American in the Vatican. He is the head of the Vatican Bank and reports directly to Pope Paul VI.

POPE PAUL VI

He is in the last few months of his pontificate.

CARDINAL PERICLE FELICI

Head of the Vatican Supreme Court. An arch-conservative who has consistently opposed the liberal policies of the Second Vatican Council.

CARDINAL ALFREDO OTTAVIANI

Over eighty, he is still one of the principal leaders of the conservative element in the Church. He was one of the cardinals responsible for convincing Paul VI to reject any form of artificial birth control.

CARDINAL SEBASTIANO BAGGIO

Prefect of the Second Congregation of Bishops, he is in charge of the Church's bishops throughout the world.

CARDINAL BERNARDIN GANTIN

Born in Africa, he is presently stationed in the Vatican because of a conflict between him and a repressive government in the Republic of Benin.

CARDINAL LEO SUENENS

Cardinal of Belgium, he is one of the great liberal figures of the Church. He was instrumental in electing Paul VI and then dared to criticize him publicly for being too conservative.

CARDINAL ALOISIO LORSCHEIDER

Cardinal of Rio de Janeiro, he is a liberal and one of the leaders of the Church in South America.

MONSIGNOR JOHN MAGEE

Secretary to Pope Paul VI and then to Pope John Paul I.

FATHER DIEGO LORENZI

Also one of Pope John Paul's secretaries.

DR RENATO BUZZONETTI

The head of the Vatican Health Service.

SISTER VINCENZA

Pope John Paul's housekeeper.

THOMAS

A Vatican gardener.

The Last Confession was first performed on 27 April 2007 at The Chichester Festival Theatre. It was subsequently toured and produced in the West End by Duncan C. Weldon and Paul Elliott for Triumph Entertainment Ltd. and Theatre Royal Haymarket Productions. The company were:

BENELLI, David Suchet

CONFESSOR, Michael Jayston

LUCIANI, Richard O'Callaghan

VILLOT, Bernard Lloyd

MARCINKUS, Stuart Milligan

POPE PAUL VI, Clifford Rose

FELICI, Charles Kay

OTTAVIANI, John Franklyn-Robbins

BAGGIO, Bruce Purchase

GANTIN, Joseph Mydell

SUENENS, Michael Cronin

LORSCHEIDER, Joseph Long

MONSIGNOR MAGEE, Roger May

FATHER LORENZI, Paul Foster

DR BUZZONETTI / THOMAS, Christopher Mellows

SISTER VINCENZA, Maroussia Frank

Director David Jones
Designer William Dudley
Costume Designer Fotini Dimou
Lighting Designer Peter Mumford
Music & Sound Designer Dominic Muldowney
Assistant Director Thomas Hescott
Casting Director Joyce Nettles
Costume Supervisor Carrie Bayliss
Production Manager Paul Hennessy
Company Manager Di Holt
Stage Manager Xenia Lewis
Deputy Stage Manager Judith Barrow
Assistant Stage Managers Jessica Cutler & Kerrie Driscoll

Act One

It is night. The room is a study. A priest about sixty years old is writing at a small table. He is of middle height. He is CARDINAL BENELLI. He is seriously ill and his movements at the beginning of the scene reflect this. A priest enters.

LORENZI: You have a visitor Your Eminence.

BENELLI: Yes. (*A grim smile of satisfaction.*) Send him in.

LORENZI hesitates for a moment, then leaves. BENELLI stands up, he seems to gain a little strength and stands taller. The CONFESSOR enters. He is dressed very simply. He is short but strongly built.

You are late.

CONFESSOR: At least, I am here. (*BENELLI stares for a moment then nods in acknowledgement.*)

BENELLI: How is Rome?

CONFESSOR: Eternal.

BENELLI: That is what we were taught.

CONFESSOR: Do you doubt it?

BENELLI: I have many doubts.

CONFESSOR: I was told you were ill.

BENELLI: I am dying.

CONFESSOR: (*Unmoved.*) Do you wish to confess?

BENELLI: What I wish for is peace.

CONFESSOR: Then confess and find peace.

BENELLI: I have. There. (*He point to a manuscript.*)

9

CONFESSOR: They told me you had written a confession and were considering publishing it.

BENELLI: Yes.

CONFESSOR: (*Disdainfully.*) Public confession is no longer in vogue in the Church. I have come to hear your private confession.

BENELLI: You have come because you had no other choice.

CONFESSOR: We have always had choices. Neither one of us has ever been afraid to make them.

BENELLI: The Church needs a public confession.

CONFESSOR: The Church needs only God.

BENELLI: And where do God's plans end and man's begin? Where is the line between divine providence and human intervention? Have you forgotten Luciani?

CONFESSOR: Yes.

BENELLI: (*Reading from the first page of the manuscript.*) 'I, Giovanni Benelli, Patriarch of Florence and Cardinal of the Roman Catholic Church, do hereby state that this is my Last Will and Testament, my final confession.' (*Turning to the CONFESSOR.*) Luciani was without doubts.

CONFESSOR: I didn't come here to talk about Luciani.

BENELLI: Then leave… (*The CONFESSOR starts to exit.*) and I will publish my confession. (*The CONFESSOR stops and looks at BENELLI for a moment.*) It begins with Luciani, it begins five years ago.

The CONFESSOR walks to a chair and sits down. He puts a stole around his neck and blesses himself. BENELLI also blesses himself.

Bless me Father for I have sinned. I have killed the Emissary of God.

The stage comes alive with priests and cardinals, hurrying about their business. Amongst them is a small short man. He is dressed as a priest but wears a gold chain and crucifix. He looks lost. A priest stops for a minute. It is MONSIGNOR MAGEE.

MAGEE: Can I help?

LUCIANI: I was looking for Archbishop Benelli.

MAGEE: Do you have an appointment?

LUCIANI: No.

MAGEE: The Archbishop may be busy…

LUCIANI: I can wait…

MAGEE: Who shall I say?

LUCIANI: Luciani, Cardinal Luciani.

MAGEE: Of course, Your Eminence, I will…

BENELLI moves across the stage to join them. As he moves he appears five years younger, vigorous and in excellent health.

BENELLI: Albino, it's good to see you. I enjoyed your book.

LUCIANI: You did? Thank you. It was just some letters.

BENELLI: Yes (*Smiling.*) but to Charles Dickens, Jules Verne… very illustrious. What brings you to Rome?

LUCIANI: I came to see His Holiness, but he is too busy. (*To MAGEE with a warm smile.*) Thank you. (*MAGEE exits.*) It must be a terrible thing to be Pope.

BENELLI: For some men.

LUCIANI: It is bad enough being a cardinal.

BENELLI: Patriarch of Venice. A beautiful city.

LUCIANI: My parishioners wanted me to have my own boat and gondolier. Can you imagine a private boat just waiting for me?

BENELLI: I've seen your car. You could do with a boat... What do you do when you need one?

LUCIANI: Call the fire brigade. They lend me one of theirs.

BENELLI: And if there is a fire?

LUCIANI: (*Smiling.*) Sometimes even God has to wait. (*Pause. Simply.*) I need help. Bishop Marcinkus is selling the Catholic Bank of Venice.

BENELLI: Yes, I know. For far less than it is worth. Have you discussed this with our Secretary of State?

LUCIANI: I did. He said he could do nothing.

BENELLI: Then Cardinal Villot is wiser than I thought.

LUCIANI: You run the Church for His Holiness, not Villot.

BENELLI: (*Enjoying the comment.*) Not many cardinals in the Curia would enjoy hearing that.

LUCIANI: You are the Pope's friend.

BENELLI: Marcinkus is his banker.

LUCIANI: And what about the poor of Venice? The Church is their banker.

BENELLI: The poor are always with us.

LUCIANI: When the Pope sent me to Venice the churches were empty but the streets were filled with prostitutes, with the mentally ill, with the handicapped. The City had shut its doors. I opened mine. I will not abandon them.

BENELLI: (*Assessing him.*) Marcinkus has dangerous friends.

LUCIANI: Are you afraid of him?

BENELLI: (*Amused.*) No.

LUCIANI: Then help us.

BENELLI: You want me to fight him over some little bank in Venice?

LUCIANI: Yes.

BENELLI: Marcinkus will hold this against you. He has used the power of the Vatican bank to break people, even cardinals.

LUCIANI: One cardinal less (*Smiling.*) especially a small one doesn't matter. Will you help?

BENELLI: (*Pause.*) Perhaps it is time I had a talk with Marcinkus. I will try.

LUCIANI: Thank you. (*LUCIANI exits.*)

CONFESSOR: I had forgotten how persistent he could be.

BENELLI: He was right.

CONFESSOR: He was naïve.

BENELLI: No... He was innocent... I met with Villot and Marcinkus, just as he had asked.

BENELLI's office in the Vatican. CARDINAL VILLOT enters. He is a tall thin man. He has strong angular features and looks every inch the cardinal. He has a slight French accent. BENELLI joins VILLOT.

VILLOT: I hope this is necessary.

BENELLI: Marcinkus is selling the Catholic Bank of Venice.

VILLOT: It has nothing to do with us.

BENELLI: He is selling it for far less than it is worth. Why?

VILLOT: (*Dismissively.*) He's an American…from Chicago. (*Turns to leave.*)

BENELLI: Cicero to be precise. The home of the gangster, Al Capone. (*VILLOT stops to look at BENELLI.*)

VILLOT: If you want to discuss Marcinkus, draft an agenda and contact my secretary. We will discuss it then.

BENELLI: We need to do something now.

VILLOT: Marcinkus has the confidence of His Holiness.

BENELLI: I thought you did too.

VILLOT: Twice on trips Marcinkus has saved the Pope's life. You can wrestle with the Pope's gorilla if you want to. I have better things to do.

BISHOP MARCINKUS enters. He is tall, six feet three inches, and powerfully built. His features are rough and he would look like a construction worker except he is dressed like a parish priest. He wears nothing that would indicate a higher office.

MARCINKUS: (*To VILLOT with a hint of condescension.*) Cardinal Villot. (*Looking at BENELLI.*) I didn't realise that we were going to have a formal meeting. (*To VILLOT.*) You should have sent me an agenda.

VILLOT: There isn't a meeting.

BENELLI: Luciani visited me today. He had some questions about the Catholic Bank of Venice.

MARCINKUS: He should have come to see me. I always enjoy the visits of cardinals.

VILLOT: (*Dryly.*) You enjoy cardinals begging for money.

MARCINKUS: Cardinals do not beg, they command. But sometimes I have to say no… (*Smiling.*) It is a terrible job.

BENELLI: Not many can say no to a cardinal.

MARCINKUS: I hear Archbishop Benelli does – often. (*To VILLOT.*) Isn't that correct Your Eminence?

BENELLI: (*Smiling.*) I say what the Pope tells me.

MARCINKUS: I thought you reported to His Eminence, the Secretary of State.

BENELLI: In the end, we must all answer to His Holiness…

MARCINKUS: And Pope Paul has placed me in charge of the Vatican Bank.

VILLOT: To lend money to religious organisations in need.

MARCINKUS: I…the bank can't help everyone, but the ones we do help are always so grateful…even cardinals.

VILLOT: What do you mean by that?

MARCINKUS: How much I am consoled by the gratitude of so many cardinals.

BENELLI: Selling religious banks is not a purpose of the Vatican Bank that I am aware of.

MARCINKUS: Raising money is. BENELLI: I hear the price Calvi is paying…is somewhat low.

MARCINKUS: These things are always so difficult to determine. Calvi is a very astute businessman. The bank relies on him frequently.

BENELLI: Calvi is in the business of high-risk finance…or that is what he calls it… That is not the business of the Vatican Bank.

MARCINKUS: Calvi has the complete confidence of myself… and of course His Holiness.

VILLOT: (*Unable to help himself.*) So did Sindona, his predecessor.

BENELLI: (*More a statement than a question.*) And where is Sindona now?

MARCINKUS: I hear he is in a cell.

VILLOT: A jail cell.

BENELLI: No doubt saying his prayers.

VILLOT: It will take more than prayers.

MARCINKUS: (*To VILLOT.*) Perhaps you would like to point out to His Holiness his error in trusting his friend Sindona?

BENELLI: Since you were placed in charge of the Vatican Bank its principal advisor has been jailed and the bank accused of participating in a multi-million dollar bond fraud.

MARCINKUS: I think 'accused' is a little strong.

BENELLI: What word would you use?

MARCINKUS: People can accuse…it is always more difficult to prove innocence than imply guilt.

BENELLI: And when the FBI paid you a visit last month?

MARCINKUS: It was a pity that I couldn't help them.

BENELLI: Perhaps I can.

MARCINKUS: This is Bank business.

BENELLI: This is Church business. I think it is time someone looked into the Bank's finances. (*BENELLI looks at VILLOT.*)

MARCINKUS: The Vatican Bank is the Pope's bank...owned by the Pope...for the Pope's purposes.

BENELLI: The Pope's purposes...not Calvi's.

MARCINKUS: Perhaps I was not clear. You may be able to make the rest of the Vatican report to you but not the Vatican Bank.

BENELLI: I will have an accounting.

MARCINKUS: I am accountable only to the Pope and to God.

Three men enter. One is POPE PAUL VI. He moves slowly because of arthritis in one knee. He is frail, thin, ascetic-looking and in his late seventies, but still every inch a Pope. He uses the royal 'we'. He has his hand on the shoulder of his secretary MONSIGNOR JOHN MAGEE for support. The third person is CARDINAL PERICLE FELICI who is in his late sixties. CARDINAL FELICI is generally smooth and charming, but the charm of a snake.

PAUL: (*With a tired smile.*) At least one of us is here.

MARCINKUS: (*Startled.*) Your Holiness.

PAUL: (*To BENELLI.*) We had a call from the bank that you were meeting with Bishop Marcinkus.

PAUL looks at MARCINKUS then at VILLOT and then at BENELLI.

(*To BENELLI.*) We see you are making friends.

BENELLI: (*Unperturbed.*) I am always trying...

PAUL: Perhaps we can be of help.

BENELLI: We were discussing finance Your Holiness.

PAUL: Bishop Marcinkus is very knowledgeable about finance.

BENELLI: He was explaining some of Calvi's subtler manoeuvres.

PAUL: Calvi is hardly subtle. (*To MARCINKUS.*) Perhaps you might enlighten us.

MARCINKUS: We are selling Calvi the Catholic Bank of Venice.

PAUL: (*Sits down in a chair and stares at MARCINKUS.*) Is that necessary?

MARCINKUS: He needs it to expand Banco Ambrosiano's asset base. That will raise its stock price so Calvi can make more acquisitions.

PAUL: Do we own Banco Ambrosiano?

VILLOT: No, Your Holiness.

MARCINKUS: A small piece.

BENELLI: A very small piece.

MARCINKUS: We have very profitable investments with Ambrosiano. If we help them, they help us.

FELICI: For an American, that sounds very Italian.

MARCINKUS: I have lived in the Vatican for some time.

PAUL: (*To BENELLI.*) It seems to be necessary. Is Luciani upset?

BENELLI: Yes.

PAUL: He is a good man. He understands that sometimes it is necessary to sacrifice… (*To MARCINKUS.*) And when were you going to tell us?

MARCINKUS: Tomorrow, Your Holiness.

BENELLI: The sale hasn't closed.

PAUL: Have we signed a contract?

MARCINKUS: Yes.

PAUL: (*To BENELLI.*) Bishop Marcinkus has our complete confidence… In financial matters.

MARCINKUS: Thank you Your Holiness. (*He kisses PAUL's ring.*)

PAUL: You may leave us.

VILLOT kisses the Pope's ring. VILLOT, MARCINKUS and MAGEE exit. PAUL holds up his hand indicating that FELICI should stay.

(*To BENELLI.*) We have been discussing the status of the new Code of Church Law with Cardinal Felici. The ever-changing, never-finished Church Law. (*To FELICI.*) It is a canon of law, not the Sistine Chapel. When will you be done?

FELICI: These things take time.

BENELLI: Ten years!

PAUL: Your Commission's latest draft is a labyrinth of rigid rules.

FELICI: A majority of the bishops approved.

BENELLI: (*Amused by the dispute.*) Fewer than half were asked.

FELICI: Is that true? I will see to it that a copy is circulated to every bishop.

BENELLI: And the direction of the Second Vatican Council, that the Canon reflect the simple teaching of the gospels?

FELICI: The gospels were inspired by God, my commission has to rely on the talents of men.

BENELLI: Perhaps someone else can provide inspiration.

FELICI: My dear Archbishop, I understand that your talents are fully employed elsewhere.

PAUL: (*To BENELLI.*) You are to communicate the comments and suggestions of the bishops to Cardinal Felici so that the commission can finish its work for our review... (*To FELICI.*) ...and the commission will finish.

FELICI: Of course.

PAUL: Benelli will help us back to our rooms. (*PAUL holds up his right hand. FELICI kisses it.*) There is only so much time...especially for us.

FELICI: (*Smiles faintly.*) I know. (*To BENELLI.*) I would be very interested in your views on the new Code. Perhaps you would be kind enough to stop by my chambers.

BENELLI: As you wish... (*FELICI leaves.*) He will never finish.

PAUL: In the end he will have to draft it as the Vatican Council directed.

BENELLI: And Marcinkus?

PAUL: We need his help just like we need yours.

BENELLI: His friend Calvi is corrupt.

PAUL: The Vatican, like any great power, needs money.

BENELLI: It is a great faith.

PAUL: It is a great power. Never doubt it. (*PAUL stands up.*) You need friends my son. Make Marcinkus a friend. He is good at helping people. (*BENELLI walks over to PAUL, and PAUL puts his arm over BENELLI's shoulder.*)

BENELLI: Not Marcinkus. (*They start to move together off stage with BENELLI helping PAUL.*)

PAUL: Be careful of power Giovanni… (*Smiling sadly.*) Your punishment may be finding it.

The two stop. PAUL looks at BENELLI for a moment. PAUL then exits. BENELLI freezes. As he does, lights come up on CARDINAL FELICI and CARDINAL OTTAVIANI. OTTAVIANI is a small man in his mid-eighties. He is still vigorous. They are in FELICI's rooms in the Vatican.

OTTAVIANI: He was a pompous fool when he was young and he's still a fool.

FELICI: He is the Pope.

OTTAVIANI: Is he going to resign when he turns eighty? Of course not. How dare he decree that cardinals over eighty cannot vote at the next conclave! And he has appointed twenty new cardinals. The best are fools like himself…the worst might as well be communists.

FELICI: Is Benelli on the list?

OTTAVIANI: No thank God. He is bad enough as an archbishop.

FELICI: I have heard that privately he disagrees with the Pope's willingness to negotiate with the communists. What are his views on Church reform, his religious views?

OTTAVIANI: The Pope's.

FELICI: And when the Pope dies?

BENELLI moves across the stage and joins them.

BENELLI: (*To FELICI.*) Your Eminence, you wanted to discuss the new Canon Law.

FELICI: We were discussing the new cardinals. I am surprised to hear that you are not on the list.

BENELLI: (*Smiling.*) As the Pope wills.

OTTAVIANI: As God wills.

FELICI: I hear that the mission to Moscow was successful and the Vatican and the Kremlin are close to a detente.

OTTAVIANI: To hell with detente.

BENELLI: His Holiness is only trying to stop the persecution of Catholics.

OTTAVIANI: Persecution is good for the soul.

BENELLI: (*Mildly.*) There is already enough blood in the mortar of the Church. (*OTTAVIANI looks BENELLI up and down.*)

FELICI: (*To OTTAVIANI.*) Perhaps you might excuse us?

OTTAVIANI: As you wish. (*To BENELLI.*) Please convey my congratulations to His Holiness.

BENELLI: On what?

OTTAVIANI: On being… (*Wanting to use another word but retraining himself.*) …consistent. (*OTTAVIANI leaves.*)

FELICI: (*Amused.*) Forgive him. He just learned he will not be voting at the next conclave. I am glad you decided to accept my invitation.

BENELLI: You have a wonderful view.

FELICI: I can see most of Rome.

BENELLI: You can also look directly into the papal apartments.

FELICI: At night I see him hard at work at his desk, caring for Mother Church.

BENELLI: His Holiness is very diligent. He eagerly awaits your revised Canon Law.

FELICI: Pope John and the Second Vatican Council said they wanted to open the windows of the Church for a dialogue with the world. What if he and the Council were wrong? What if they let something else in…doubt…uncertainty…division…

BENELLI: You mean reassessment…renewal.

FELICI: Men need to reassess. Men need renewal. The Church is. Truth is. Reassessing doesn't change them.

BENELLI: Even the Church can need renewal.

FELICI: Are the articles of faith enunciated by Christ any different if placed in the context of history or analysed by modern sociology? No, they are unchanging, eternal.

BENELLI: Men change. How they view the world changes. You and I change.

FELICI: Men are not the measure of truth. God is.

BENELLI: How do you measure God?

FELICI: Against two thousand years of tradition.

BENELLI: The Vatican Council has directed you to embody the spirit of the gospels in the new canon.

FELICI: The gospels are a beautiful ideal, impossible to realise in the present world. (*Pause.*) How do you reconcile your exercise of power with the simple life of Christ?

BENELLI: I pray, Your Eminence, I have not forgotten how to pray.

FELICI: And has God answered you?

BENELLI: God has given me the questions...he will help me find the answers.

FELICI: You would make a good Lutheran.

BENELLI: Then so would the Pope.

FELICI: Our Hamlet Pope.

BENELLI: Are you saying the Holy Father is in error?

FELICI: We need a Pope great enough to be ruthless in the defence of Christ's Church. You could be such a Pope.

BENELLI: We have a Pope.

FELICI: The Pope is old.

BENELLI: His health is good.

FELICI: Is it? Soon, very soon we will elect a new Pope. (*FELICI walks to the edge of the stage.*) The man who lives in those apartments is the Vicar of Christ on earth. He holds the allegiance of eight hundred million Catholics and the respect of hundreds of millions more. Governments fear his judgement. Kings have knelt down before him. (*BENELLI joins FELICI at the window.*) I can make you Pope.

BENELLI: (*Quietly.*) Only God can make a Pope.

FELICI: Cardinals make Popes.

BENELLI: (*Still quiet.*) And Satan took Jesus to the highest mountain and showed him all the kingdoms of the earth… I serve the Pope.

FELICI: Your service is to God.

BENELLI: And I will listen to Him when He calls. Until then both of us serve the Pope. You will finish the canon.

FELICI: I will revise the canon. It will be interesting to see if you are still here when I am done.

The lights go down on BENELLI and FELICI and come up on the Pope's study. Present are PAUL, VILLOT, MAGEE and CARDINAL SEBASTIANO BAGGIO. BAGGIO is a stocky, self-important man in his early sixties.

VILLOT: The next item for your consideration is our negotiations with the Russians.

PAUL: We have agreed not to actively oppose them.

VILLOT: The Kremlin now wants a public statement that communism can be compatible with the Catholic Church.

PAUL: Our silence should be enough. Benelli thinks even that is too much. Tell the Kremlin that we will not speak out against them. That is all we can do for now.

VILLOT: And in the future?

PAUL: Suggest there is the possibility that we might do more to help – the possibility, no more.

VILLOT: Which brings us to the last item: Benelli. At our last meeting you agreed to consider the idea of a transfer. I have drafted a list of possible new positions.

PAUL: We agreed to consider it. (*VILLOT hands PAUL the list.*)

VILLOT: I have discussed the matter with Felici and Marcinkus. They also agree that the Archbishop would serve the Church better elsewhere.

PAUL: We see that you have picked some interesting locations. Zambia, Borneo, Paraguay…

VILLOT: The Curia was very helpful in making suggestions.

PAUL: Why?

VILLOT: Benelli's presence has become detrimental to the smooth running of the Curia.

PAUL: The Curia has never run smoothly, at least not in our lifetime.

VILLOT: (*Pompously.*) The Vatican is like a family, and like a family it can stand a certain amount of discord. But there comes a point where the divisions are so great that it can no longer function.

PAUL: We didn't know that you had become an expert on families.

VILLOT: I am an expert on government.

PAUL: We thought we were all here to serve God.

VILLOT: Cardinal Baggio agrees.

PAUL: You too.

BAGGIO: He can be difficult, Your Holiness.

PAUL: Usually when Benelli is difficult there is a reason.

BAGGIO: I will not have some archbishop tell me what to do.

PAUL: (*Mildly.*) Who is Pope here?

BAGGIO: That is the point! Benelli seems to have forgotten.

VILLOT: If Benelli stays, then I resign.

PAUL: Be careful, we may accept. (*To BAGGIO.*) And you, are you resigning as well?

BAGGIO: (*Shocked.*) No.

PAUL: (*To VILLOT.*) We do not accept your resignation.

VILLOT: And Benelli?

PAUL: (*Reluctantly.*) We will talk to him.

> *VILLOT, BAGGIO and MAGEE exit. PAUL stands with difficulty and walks to the windows at the side of the stage. BENELLI enters.*

BENELLI: Your Holiness.

PAUL: (*Not looking at him.*) How long have we been Pope?

BENELLI: Fourteen years.

PAUL: The newspapers write about us in the past tense. It is strange to read about ourselves as if we were already dead. We have accomplished so little.

BENELLI: There is still time.

PAUL: We were elected to heal the divisions in the Church. Now it is more divided than ever. Birth control, divorce, abortion, priests wanting to marry, women wanting to be priests, thousands of priests giving up their vocations and leaving the Church. Even the authority of the Pope is questioned...We have become the obstacle to Church unity.

BENELLI: You have made the Church the servant of the people.

PAUL: The Church we were born to was the servant of God.

BENELLI: You are the Pope. Take back your Church. Throw out anyone in the Curia who will not support you. Reach out to your people...reach out to them.

PAUL: We are seventy-nine years old. (*PAUL walks slowly to his desk and sits.*) Someone else will have to try. Whoever next sits in this chair. Pope John told us that the Curia defeats every Pope in the end. He was right... My son, you will have to leave us. You will have to leave Rome.

BENELLI: I need to be here.

PAUL: You must go.

BENELLI: I can't.

PAUL: (*Gently.*) Will you disobey us?

BENELLI: Villot has been trying to exile me for years. Who else?

PAUL: Felici, Marcinkus, all of them.

BENELLI: (*Pause.*) And if I say no?

PAUL: Everything here is over. All that is left is our death. The future is for the next Pope. We have appointed twenty new cardinals, mostly foreign. The Roman Curia will not be able to control the next conclave. And they hate us for it. (*Pause.*) Who will come after us? Villot?

BENELLI: No, he is too weak.

PAUL: Pignedoli?

BENELLI: A lightweight.

PAUL: Baggio?

BENELLI: A shallow opportunist.

PAUL: Felici?

BENELLI: Anyone other than Felici.

PAUL: What about you?

BENELLI: Cardinals become Pope, not archbishops.

PAUL: We can make you a cardinal.

BENELLI: Then me, before Felici.

PAUL: Today we will announce that we have appointed you cardinal and assigned you to Florence. Will you go?

BENELLI: Yes.

PAUL: (*Sitting back in his chair.*) At least you have not failed us. But we fear we have failed God.

BENELLI: You are a great Pope.

PAUL: (*Pause.*) I wonder, when I stand before God and account for my stewardship of His Holy Church, how will I be judged?

BENELLI: With mercy.

PAUL: Go to Florence, Cardinal Benelli. Go with our blessing. (*BENELLI kneels and PAUL blesses him. Then BENELLI kisses PAUL's ring.*) But, remember one thing, men do not chose a Pope, God does. (*BENELLI stands and starts to leave.*) Giovanni... (*BENELLI stops and looks at PAUL.*) Pray for me.

The light on PAUL dims but does not go out completely. BENELLI is joined by the CONFESSOR.

CONFESSOR: You, not Felici... Why?

BENELLI: (*To the CONFESSOR.*) Because I saw in him my worst self. I wanted to be Pope. I burned to be Pope... But... How could I reconcile this use of power with the life of Christ?

CONFESSOR: There is nothing wrong with the use of power in the name of God.

BENELLI: I am talking about pride, overwhelming arrogance. The belief that you can mold history to your own design.

CONFESSOR: To know you are right, to do what is right is not wrong. Christ's Church needs to be protected.

BENELLI: And who protects his people from the Church?

CONFESSOR: God acts through men. Without power there is persecution. Shall I tell you about persecution, about what it is like to go to sleep each night, wondering if you will wake up in prison? Where every man is a betrayer and the only truth is the belief nourished in your heart.

BENELLI: Truth…Pope Paul believed that truth is found only through suffering. I have found only emptiness… Somewhere beneath the marbled dome of the Vatican, somewhere in the countless bureaucratic struggles, my faith had slipped away.

CONFESSOR: You abandoned God?

BENELLI: I think God abandoned me… (*BENELLI looks at PAUL for a moment. The light on PAUL goes out.*) On August the sixth, nineteen seventy-eight, at nine forty p.m. Pope Paul VI, the two hundred and sixtieth direct successor of Peter, as God's representative on earth, died. He was eighty years old. He had reigned fifteen years, one month and fifteen days. He was my friend. (*The lights narrow down on BENELLI. Bells peal in the background.*) And the message went out across the world to the cardinal princes of the Roman Catholic Church, the Pope is dead. You are summoned to the conclave, summoned to elect the next Pope and to decide the fate of the Catholic Church. Not the Holy Spirit, but, I, Cardinal Giovanni Benelli would select the next Pope, a gentler holy man, a man without doubts, too humble to be changed by power.

CONFESSOR: An innocent!

BENELLI: Perhaps… I would select the next Pope, and God help the cardinals in the Vatican on my return.

The lights on BENELLI expand. BENELLI has been joined by CARDINAL LEO SUENENS. They are in the Vatican. SUENENS is from Brussels and is in his mid-seventies.

SUENENS: You should have stayed in Rome after the funeral. You missed all the fun.

BENELLI: I accomplished more, Cardinal Suenens, in Florence using the telephone.

SUENENS: But it couldn't have been nearly as interesting. Every night Pignedoli has a different group of cardinals over to dinner. His thinking may be lightweight but his wine cellar is outstanding and he has one of the best chefs in Rome.

BENELLI: I don't think even Pignedoli can cook his way to the Papacy.

SUENENS: The London bookmakers have published odds on a number of candidates. Pignedoli is the favorite, so perhaps they don't share your views on his chef. Siri is second, Felici is third – he claims he supports Siri – and you are listed fourth at four to one.

BENELLI: And Luciani?

SUENENS: Who?

BENELLI: Luciani – Patriarch of Venice.

SUENENS: Not listed, of course. They have me down at thirty-three to one. (*SUENENS laughs.*)

BENELLI: So much for publicly criticising Pope Paul.

SUENENS: I couldn't wait for reforms any longer. And then there is CREEP...

BENELLI: What is creep?

SUENENS: Committee for the Responsible Election of the Pope.

BENELLI: I assume it doesn't include any cardinals.

SUENENS: Correct... Listen to their criteria. (*SUENENS takes out a piece of paper and reads from it.*) 'Help wanted. A hopeful, holy man who can smile. (*Looking up.*) That's the heading. (*Continuing reading.*) And it goes on. A man free from any sign of wheeling and dealing.'

BENELLI: Perhaps you should apply?

SUENENS: I still enjoy the wheeling and dealing.

BENELLI: They have described Luciani.

SUENENS: You can't be serious? (*Pause.*) When I supported Paul at the last conclave at least I knew he wanted to be Pope. The press asked Luciani yesterday. He told them, 'You can't make gnocchi out of this dough.'

BENELLI: Humility used to be a virtue in the church.

SUENENS: He knows himself. He won't accept.

BENELLI: If the conclave votes for him, he will accept.

CARDINAL GANTIN enters. He is African, in his early fifties and currently stationed at the Vatican due to political tensions with the Republic of Benin.

32

GANTIN: (*To BENELLI.*) Your Eminence. (*GANTIN bows respectfully to BENELLI.*) Cardinal Suenens. (*GANTIN's bow is little more than a nod of his head.*)

SUENENS: (*Nodding back.*) Cardinal Gantin.

GANTIN: (*To SUENENS.*) Playing politics again? The Holy Spirit will decide who is to be the next Pope.

SUENENS: Sometimes the Holy Spirit needs help.

GANTIN: (*To BENELLI.*) My brother cardinals in Africa agree. They asked me to come and see you. (*Pause.*) Baggio met recently with Marcinkus. He told Marcinkus that if he becomes Pope he will keep him in charge of the Vatican Bank.

BENELLI: Are you certain?

GANTIN: In the Vatican everything is confidential and nothing is secret.

BENELLI: If you oppose Baggio, Marcinkus can cut off funding for the African dioceses.

GANTIN: Africa is used to poverty. The reactionaries are organising around Felici and Siri.

BENELLI: What do you want from me?

GANTIN: My brother cardinals and I want to know if you are willing to become more than a cardinal.

BENELLI: (*Pause.*) I am too young for consideration.

SUENENS: (*To GANTIN.*) That is what he told me.

GANTIN: These are special times; they may demand a young Pope.

SUENENS: He has this thing about the Church needing a holy pastor.

GANTIN: What we need is a Christ to drive the money-lenders from the temple.

BENELLI: (*Smiling.*) Christ was also a holy pastor.

GANTIN: Will you reconsider?

BENELLI: What do you want in the next Pope?

GANTIN: A man of strength.

BENELLI: (*Softly, pleased with the implicit compliment.*) Yes.

GANTIN: Of integrity.

BENELLI: Yes.

GANTIN: Of compassion.

BENELLI: (*Silence.*) Have you met Cardinal Luciani?

GANTIN: Briefly.

BENELLI: He has written a series of letters to historic figures such as Dickens, Mark Twain, Marie Antoinette. Each letter makes a simple, moral point. They have been published in a book.

GANTIN: I have heard something about it.

BENELLI: You and your friends should read Luciani's book.

GANTIN: That's all you want me to tell them.

BENELLI: And that I am voting for him.

GANTIN: I will tell them.

> *GANTIN bows respectfully to BENELLI, nods to SUENENS and leaves.*

SUENENS: The Holy Spirit will decide. (*He shakes his head.*)
Why won't you let us support you?

BENELLI: No.

SUENENS: A reluctance for power has never been one of your
virtues.

BENELLI: Perhaps I don't care to stand that close to God...

*The lights dim slightly. Groups of cardinals enter the stage talking
and gesturing to each other. The lights brighten on BENELLI
and SUENENS. Two cardinals stop and bow respectfully to
BENELLI, then move on. The conclave has begun. VILLOT steps
to a table. CARDINAL FELICI hands him a basket containing
the votes.*

VILLOT: The first ballot has been collected. (*He pulls one out
and starts reading it aloud.*) A vote for Cardinal Felici, a vote
for Cardinal Siri, a vote for Cardinal Luciani, a vote for
Cardinal Benelli...

SUENENS: Luciani has twenty votes, Siri has twenty-five and
Pignedoli has dropped to fifteen. Baggio has nine. You
have twenty. They are still voting for you – despite what
you said. If you can get Pignedoli to release his supporters
and swing the South Americans from Lorscheider to you...

BENELLI: I've already spoken to Pignedoli.

SUENENS: What did you tell him?

BENELLI: That his dream of becoming Pope was over, that for
the good of the Church he had to support Luciani.

SUENENS: How did he take it?

BENELLI: Not well, but he knows I have a long memory. He
has agreed to ask his supporters to vote for Luciani.

SUENENS: You can't intimidate Lorscheider. Even the Brazilian death squads couldn't do that.

BENELLI: I wouldn't want to.

SUENENS: How is Luciani?

BENELLI: Shaken. When I left him he was in his room praying. Find Gantin...go and talk to him.

SUENENS: What shall we tell him?

BENELLI: That it is the will of God.

A moment after SUENENS leaves, CARDINAL ALOISO LORSCHEIDER enters. LORSCHEIDER is in his mid-fifties. He bows respectfully to BENELLI.

LORSCHEIDER: Your Eminence.

BENELLI: Cardinal Lorscheider, I am glad to see you. Cardinal Luciani thinks it may be time for a non-Italian Pope.

LORSCHEIDER: The Papacy has been Italian for five hundred years. One might think it is time for a change.

BENELLI: He is telling the cardinals that you should be Pope.

LORSCHEIDER: I know.

As they talk they walk about nodding to the other cardinals, most of whom nod respectfully back.

BENELLI: What do you think of Luciani?

LORSCHEIDER: He visited me in Rio last year. He is a charming and gentle man, more knowledgeable than some people believe. But, he is no administrator.

BENELLI: You have said the next Pope should be a holy man, a good pastor, a man of hope. You have described Luciani.

LORSCHEIDER: He would need a strong Secretary of State.

BENELLI: Yes.

LORSCHEIDER: Felici is saying that he may switch his support to Luciani. South America cannot accept a Pope guided by Felici.

BENELLI: Felici cannot control Luciani. He is a simple man. But it is the kind of simplicity that sees directly into the heart of issues, directly into men's souls.

LORSCHEIDER: I would support you.

BENELLI: I am not a candidate.

LORSCHEIDER: Luciani does not want to be a candidate.

BENELLI: Have you heard that the first test-tube baby was recently born in England?

LORSCHEIDER: Yes.

BENELLI: Many church leaders condemned the birth.

LORSCHEIDER: I know.

BENELLI: I would like to read you a letter from Cardinal Luciani. (*BENELLI takes out a paper, reading.*) 'I send the most heartfelt congratulations to the English baby girl whose conception took place artificially. As far as her parents are concerned I have no right to condemn them. If they acted with honest intentions and in good faith, they may even have great merit before God for what they wanted and asked the doctors to carry out.' (*There is a moment's silence.*)

LORSCHEIDER: He is still no match for Felici, Baggio and the rest of the Curia.

BENELLI: You are wrong. Yes he is gentle, yes he is humble, and he can take a long time to make up his mind, sometimes, too long…but when he is committed to a course of action he is like a rock.

LORSCHEIDER: You are his friend (*LORSCHEIDER and BENELLI look directly into each other's eyes.*) Promise me you will protect him from Felici and the rest of the Curia.

BENELLI: I promise.

LORSCHEIDER: (*Holds out his hand.*) Will you give me the letter? I think some of the other cardinals would like to read it.

BENELLI hands LORSCHEIDER the letter. BENELLI stands up and he and LORSCHEIDER walk up stage. LORSCHEIDER walks over to some of the other cardinals and hands them the letter. They look at it. More cardinals enter including VILLOT, BAGGIO, SUENENS, FELICI and LUCIANI. The cardinals gather at the back of the stage. The cardinals standing on either side of LUCIANI are LORSCHEIDER and GANTIN. CARDINAL FELICI hands VILLOT a paper.

VILLOT: (*Reading from the paper.*) The ballots have been tallied. Cardinal Luciani has received sixty-eight votes, Cardinal Siri fifteen votes. No other candidate has received more than two votes. I suggest that we immediately conduct a fourth ballot. Do you agree?

The cardinals all nod their heads. One or two say 'agreed'.

LUCIANI: (*He bows his head and says softly.*) No. Please no.

LORSCHEIDER: (*He grips LUCIANI's arm.*) If the Lord gives the burden, he also gives the strength to carry it.

GANTIN: (*He grips LUCIANI's other arm.*) The whole world prays for a new Pope.

The lights go down except for a spotlight on LUCIANI. VILLOT's voice can be heard from the darkness stage-right counting the ballots.

VILLOT: A vote for Cardinal Luciani, a vote for Cardinal Luciani, a vote for Cardinal Luciani... Cardinal Luciani... (*There is silence.*) The final tally is: ninety-nine votes for Cardinal Luciani, one vote for Cardinal Lorscheider, eleven abstentions. (*The spotlight around LUCIANI expands slightly. VILLOT steps into it in front of LUCIANI. In a commanding voice.*) Do you accept your election as Supreme Pontiff?

There is a long moment of silence as LUCIANI slowly raises his head and looks at VILLOT.

LUCIANI: (*With a soft voice.*) May God forgive you for what you have done. (*Another pause. Then in a slightly louder voice.*) I accept.

VILLOT: By what name do you wish to be called?

LUCIANI: (*A short pause. LUCIANI smiles.*) John Paul the First.

A light has come up on BENELLI and the CONFESSOR. LUCIANI moves to centre stage. FELICI and VILLOT walk up to LUCIANI and dress him in the robes of the Pope. They hand him a white cap. He takes off his red cap and replaces it with the white one but puts it at rakish angle. The papal robes are noticeably too big for him. FELICI and VILLOT step back.

BENELLI: John Paul...I wonder how it feels. (*The CONFESSOR looks at him.*) Well...envy is only a little sin.

CONFESSOR: Why Luciani? Even the robes didn't fit.

BENELLI: They made the papal garments in every size... except his. Nobody had his measure.

SUENENS: (*Approaching JOHN PAUL.*) Holy Father, thank you for saying yes.

LUCIANI: Perhaps it would have been better if I had said no.

VILLOT and FELICI walk with LUCIANI to the front of the stage. FELICI steps forward.

FELICI: (*To the audience.*) I bring you news of great joy. We have a Pope, Cardinal Albino Luciani, who has chosen the name John Paul the First.

LUCIANI steps forward with a humble but radiating smile. While LUCIANI talks, the lights narrow down on him, although the light remains on the CONFESSOR and BENELLI.

LUCIANI: This morning I went to the Sistine to vote peacefully. I never imagined what was to take place. Realise this: I do not have the wisdom or heart of Pope John. Nor do I have the preparation and culture of Pope Paul. However I stand now in their place. I will seek to serve the Church and I hope that you will help me with your prayers.

BENELLI: (*To the CONFESSOR.*) Prayers were the only help he ever received.

LUCIANI blesses the audience and the lights go down. BENELLI and the CONFESSOR remain illuminated and watch what takes place. Lights come up on a nun who is busy taking books out of boxes, dusting them and then placing them on shelves in the Pope's study. Her name is SISTER VINCENZA. She is in her sixties and has been LUCIANI's housekeeper for over twenty years. With her are VILLOT and FELICI. FATHER DIEGO LORENZI enters. He is about thirty and wears glasses.

VILLOT: (*To LORENZI.*) Who are you?

LORENZI: Father Lorenzi, Your Eminence. (*VILLOT assesses LORENZI for a moment.*) I was the Holy Father's secretary when he was a cardinal in Venice.

VILLOT: (*Astonished.*) He brought you to Rome?

LORENZI: Yes, Your Eminence.

VILLOT: Where is His Holiness?

LORENZI: He said he wanted to go for a walk around the Vatican and perhaps into Rome.

VILLOT: (*Disbelief.*) He went for a walk.

VINCENZA: Father Albino always goes for a walk after his siesta in the afternoon.

VILLOT: (*To FELICI.*) This is impossible.

FELICI: (*To LORENZI.*) We need to find the Holy Father. The Pope is not supposed to wander about by himself.

VILLOT: (*To LORENZI.*) Rome is a separate country from the Vatican. If he simply walks there without proper notice and an escort it could cause a diplomatic incident. (*Thinking.*) And the mayor of Rome is a communist.

LORENZI: I don't think he intended to see the mayor.

FELICI: (*Picking up a book from the Pope's desk.*) 'On Being a Christian...'

VILLOT: (*Looking up strangely.*) What?

FELICI: 'On Being a Christian, by Dr Hans Kung'.

VILLOT: Kung?!

FELICI: (*Mildly.*) Yes. (*He opens the cover of the book.*) It is an autographed copy...with a note congratulating Cardinal

Luciani on the publication of his book, 'Illustrissimi', and thanks Luciani for sending him a copy.

VILLOT: The Pope is missing and now you tell me he is corresponding with heretics!

JOHN PAUL enters. He is dressed simply in an old cassock. His skull-cap is more on the side of his head than on top. It is generally in this position even when he is formally dressed. FELICI puts the book he is holding back in the box.

Your Holiness, where have you been?

JOHN PAUL: About.

FELICI: It might not be safe.

JOHN PAUL: Who would want to harm the Pope?

FELICI: Many people, I'm afraid, Your Holiness.

VILLOT: At the very least you should have the Swiss guard with you.

JOHN PAUL: Please tell the Commander of the guards that they are not to kneel when I talk to them.

VILLOT: You spoke to the guards?

JOHN PAUL: I wanted to know what they thought of the Vatican. (*To VINCENZA.*) Can you find us some coffee?

VINCENZA: Yes Father. (*VINCENZA exits.*)

FELICI: Your Holiness, we came to discuss the details of your coronation.

JOHN PAUL: I have been thinking about that, too. The coronation ceremony needs to be rewritten.

VILLOT: It has not changed for hundreds of years.

JOHN PAUL: (*Softly.*) There will be no crowning.

VILLOT: Impossible...the Pope is always crowned.

JOHN PAUL: I am a priest, not a king. There will be no crown... And I will walk into Saint Peter's.

FELICI: The Pope is always carried by eight men in a throne on a platform...

JOHN PAUL: (*Gently.*) I will not be carried on the backs of men.

VINCENZA enters with a tray of coffee. She is helped by MONSIGNOR MAGEE.

VINCENZA: The kitchen sent up some coffee. I tasted it Father, it's terrible. Shall I send it back?

JOHN PAUL: No thank you, Sister. We will make do.

VILLOT: Sister Vincenza should really refer to you as Your Holiness or Holy Father.

JOHN PAUL: Sister Vincenza has very fixed views. I would not change them for the world.

VILLOT: Holy Father, you should use the royal 'we' when you speak.

JOHN PAUL: (*Slightly irritated.*) I am a priest. I will speak as a priest. (*To MAGEE.*) And who are you?

VILLOT: Your Holiness, this is Monsignor Magee. I thought you had been introduced.

JOHN PAUL: I don't think we have...have we?

FELICI: He was one of Pope Paul's secretaries. He is familiar with the procedures and protocols of the Vatican.

VILLOT: And how Pope Paul handled things.

JOHN PAUL: I will need all the help I can get. Will your old room be alright?

MAGEE: Of course, Your Holiness.

JOHN PAUL: Good.

MAGEE and LORENZI leave.

(*Pouring coffee for VILLOT and FELICI.*) What else would you like to discuss?

VILLOT: (*Consulting an agenda.*) There is a request for an audience. The United States Congressional Committee on Population has requested a meeting with Your Holiness.

JOHN PAUL: When would they like to meet?

VILLOT: That is the problem. If you meet it will send the wrong message to Catholics around the world.

JOHN PAUL: I don't understand.

VILLOT: The Committee supports artificial birth control.

JOHN PAUL stands and picks up a rolled map and starts to spread it across his desk.

JOHN PAUL: This is a map of the world. (*As he puts a book at each end of the map to hold it flat, the two cardinals join him.*) There are Catholics in almost every country of the world. This year the world population reached four point four billion. Over the next year seventy-three million children will be born, most of them in the Third World. Every hour one thousand children under the age of five die of malnutrition. By this time tomorrow thirty-thousand children will be dead. Yes I will meet with the committee.

VILLOT: Is your Holiness suggesting that Pope Paul's encyclical on birth control is wrong?

JOHN PAUL: Pope Paul did not invoke the doctrine of papal infallibility when he signed the encyclical. The issue needs further study.

FELICI: The issue was studied.

JOHN PAUL: And the report of ninety per cent of the commission favored permitting some form of artificial birth control. Pope Paul was talked into rejecting the commission's report. I am not bound by his decision. (*To VILLOT.*) I want a report on every Third World country that has Catholics and I want it before I meet with the congressional committee.

VILLOT: That will take months.

JOHN PAUL: I intend to meet with the committee as soon as possible. There are three thousand employees in the Curia. Use whoever you need.

CARDINAL BENELLI leaves the CONFESSOR and joins them.

BENELLI: Holy Father. (*He approaches the Pope and kisses his ring.*)

JOHN PAUL: Cardinal Benelli, thank you for coming.

BENELLI: (*To JOHN PAUL.*) Am I interrupting?

JOHN PAUL: No.

FELICI: (*Excusing himself pointedly.*) We can talk about the coronation later.

VILLOT: (*To JOHN PAUL.*) I am certain you will think differently after we talk.

VILLOT and FELICI leave.

JOHN PAUL: This was your doing.

BENELLI: It was God's will.

JOHN PAUL: Why did you do it?

BENELLI: I am sorry, I couldn't think of anyone else.

JOHN PAUL: Not even yourself?

BENELLI: Especially not myself. Is it so terrible to be Pope?

JOHN PAUL: Yes – and the coffee's terrible, too. Would you like a cup?

BENELLI: No thank you.

LORENZI and MAGEE enter carrying papal vestments.

LORENZI: Your Holiness, it is time to get ready for your first general audience.

JOHN PAUL and BENELLI stand up, and LORENZI and MAGEE start dressing JOHN PAUL in the Pope's formal robes.

JOHN PAUL: (*To BENELLI.*) Would you like to come with me?

BENELLI: Of course.

JOHN PAUL: It is just a simple talk (*Smiling.*) but at least people will understand what the Pope has to say. Certainly I am too small for great things. But I can repeat the truth and the call of the Gospel as I did when I was a priest in my little church at home. Men need that.

BENELLI: Albino, you are the Keeper of Souls.

JOHN PAUL: If God wills.

JOHN PAUL exits with MAGEE and LORENZI, and BENELLI joins the CONFESSOR.

BENELLI: He went out and spoke to his people. He talked to children, to the old, to the infirm. He spoke to them of charity, of justice, of love, with simple stories, much as a fisherman did once, so very long ago.

CONFESSOR: I know, I was there.

BENELLI: It was as if a thousand years of dust and ceremonies had vanished overnight. And the people, the people loved him for it. They came by the thousands and knelt at the feet of this priest who was less than a Pope and more than Pope. And the more they loved him, the more those nearest in power began to fear him. And as I watched, I began to wonder what had happened in that conclave. I began to feel a sense...of purpose.

CONFESSOR: It reaffirmed your belief in God.

BENELLI: I began to believe in man. One week later the coronation ceremony took place. Except it was no longer a coronation. The ceremony, over a thousand years old, was completely rewritten. The three-crowned tiara was gone.

JOHN PAUL enters in his formal dress, either from the opposite side of stage or, if possible, through one of the aisles of the theatre. He is wearing a simple cloth miter on his head and he is followed at a small distance by his cardinals. First FELICI, then VILLOT and then the others.

In its place, he wore a simple cloth miter, the symbol of pastoral authority. Three hundred thousand people had come to see their new Pope. Ordinary men, as well as presidents and kings. For a thousand years, the Pope had been carried on a throne to the sound of trumpets. The throne was gone, the trumpets were silent, instead he came on foot, through his people.

LUCIANI and the cardinals have reached the stage. There is an altar centre stage. Behind the altar are the vast doors that lead into Saint Peter's. They can be simple and more suggestive than the actual doors. The cardinals walk to either side of the altar except for JOHN PAUL, FELICI and VILLOT who walk up to the altar. A separate, narrow spotlight remains fixed on BENELLI and the CONFESSOR. JOHN PAUL takes off the miter and hands it to FELICI. FELICI approaches the altar, places the miter on it and picks up the pallium. He turns to JOHN PAUL and places it around his neck.

FELICI: Blessed be God, Who has chosen you to be pastor of the Universal Church and Who has clothed you with the shining stole of your apostolate. May you reign gloriously through many years of earthly light until called by your Lord. You will be reclothed with the stole of immortality in the Kingdom of Heaven. Amen.

FELICI steps away from JOHN PAUL, who is now isolated. JOHN PAUL turns and blesses the audience. VILLOT approaches, kneels and kisses the papal ring. As he rises, JOHN PAUL embraces him. FELICI approaches JOHN PAUL. He stands for a moment and stares at BENELLI then he turns, kneels before JOHN PAUL and kisses his ring. As he stands, JOHN PAUL embraces him. FELICI steps away and the spotlight narrows on JOHN PAUL. JOHN PAUL turns and walks towards the doors at the back of the stage.

BENELLI: He left on foot and walked alone into Saint Peter's. And I thought the Church would never be, could never be, the same. (*JOHN PAUL exits through the doors. The lights go out.*)

The Pope's study. JOHN PAUL enters angrily. He is carrying a newspaper. There are large piles of paper on his desk. He is followed by LORENZI, who is carrying more papers.

JOHN PAUL: The Vatican press has changed my speech again. 'We' this, 'we' that; I never use 'we'. This isn't my speech. This is just official statements drafted by the Curia. They even have me celebrating the tenth anniversary of Paul's encyclical against birth control. Villot and Felici know I intend to reexamine the issue.

LORENZI: There is also an article condemning the birth of the recent test-tube baby.

JOHN PAUL: They know about the letter I wrote congratulating the baby. (*Angry.*) Damn them.

LORENZI: Holy Father.

JOHN PAUL: Forgive me, Diego. (*Smiling.*) Just a figure of speech. (*BENELLI and GANTIN enter.*)

GANTIN: (*Bowing.*) Your Holiness.

BENELLI: Holy Father. (*Noting the paper.*) Are you enjoying the latest issue of the Vatican press?

JOHN PAUL: I told Villot and Felici that this sort of thing has to stop.

GANTIN: Welcome to the Vatican, Your Holiness.

BENELLI: Sometimes they can be a little hard of hearing.

JOHN PAUL: One day very soon they will hear me. Cardinal Gantin, it is a pleasure to see you. Did Benelli tell you why I wanted to meet?

GANTIN: Yes, to talk about running the Church's organisation for international aid.

JOHN PAUL: Are you interested?

GANTIN: No.

JOHN PAUL: (*Surprised.*) Why not?

GANTIN: I will not be a party to a system that generates income through exploitation.

JOHN PAUL: (*Softly rebuking.*) You are talking about our Church.

GANTIN: And the Church should use its resources to help people learn the skills necessary for economic independence, not for investment in corporations whose purposes are incompatible with the teachings of the Church.

JOHN PAUL: (*Beginning to smile.*) I am not asking you to manage the Church's assets. I am only asking you to take charge of international aid.

GANTIN: As long as Marcinkus runs the Vatican Bank and Villot the Treasury, nothing will change.

JOHN PAUL: Things will change. (*To GANTIN.*) But, in the meantime, I need your help.

BENELLI: And Marcinkus and...

JOHN PAUL: Marcinkus and Villot are my problem. (*To GANTIN.*) As a personal favour to me, I would like you to accept.

GANTIN: Your Holiness... I accept.

JOHN PAUL: (*Smiling.*) Good. This afternoon I will tell Cardinal Villot that you are taking over his responsibilities for international aid.

JOHN PAUL holds out his hand. GANTIN kisses his ring and leaves.

(*To BENELLI.*) You suggested the right man. (*MAGEE enters.*)

MAGEE: Bishop Marcinkus is waiting to see you.

JOHN PAUL: Send him in. (*MAGEE leaves.*)

BENELLI: Do you have Villot's report on the bank?

JOHN PAUL: No. The report is important. But more important is the man. (*MARCINKUS enters.*)

MARCINKUS: Your Holiness, thank you for seeing me. (*To BENELLI.*) How is Florence?

BENELLI: Beautiful. But it is always a pleasure to visit Rome.

MARCINKUS: I'm sure your diocese misses you.

JOHN PAUL: Why don't you sit down, Bishop. (*They all sit.*) Would you like some coffee?

MARCINKUS: No, thank you.

JOHN PAUL: I understand you are from Cicero, Illinois.

MARCINKUS: (*Glancing first at BENELLI.*) Yes.

JOHN PAUL: That's near Chicago.

MARCINKUS: Yes.

JOHN PAUL: How long have you been in Rome?

MARCINKUS: Almost twenty years.

JOHN PAUL: You must miss Chicago. Do you still have family there?

MARCINKUS: A few relatives… I try to visit them whenever I can.

JOHN PAUL: It is unfortunate that the Church has kept you away from home for so long.

MARCINKUS: It is in the service of God.

JOHN PAUL: What do you do at the bank?

MARCINKUS: (*Pause.*) I set policy.

JOHN PAUL: What is the policy?

MARCINKUS: The policy (*He shrugs and smiles.*) is to make money.

BENELLI: Is that why you sold the Catholic Bank of Venice for less than it was worth?

MARCINKUS: We...the Church received other favours in exchange. If you simply invest with a bank...

BENELLI: (*Interrupting.*) Banco Ambrosiano.

MARCINKUS: For instance, Ambrosiano; if you simply invest, you receive one interest rate, a low interest rate. But if you know people at the bank they will tell you if they have a particular project, and if you earmark your money for the project, they will give you a higher rate.

JOHN PAUL: But, what about the nature of the project?

MARCINKUS: I don't ask.

BENELLI: Don't you think the Church should be concerned about the nature of its investments?

MARCINKUS: Roberto Calvi is one of Italy's cleverest businessmen. Pope Paul trusted him completely.

BENELLI: And Sindona? Pope Paul trusted him, too.

MARCINKUS: Pope Paul made a mistake with Sindona. It happens.

JOHN PAUL: I am all too aware of the fallibility of Popes.

MARCINKUS: Only in financial matters, Your Holiness.

BENELLI: Perhaps you can tell His Holiness about your investments with Calvi?

MARCINKUS: They are very complex.

JOHN PAUL: I wonder if it is wise to make such investments?

MARCINKUS: Foreign banks do it all the time.

JOHN PAUL: The Church is not a bank.

MARCINKUS: It is supported by the bank, and the bank's function is to make money.

JOHN PAUL: This is the house of God, not the house of Rothschild.

MARCINKUS: You can't run the Church on Hail Marys. (*Pause.*) Your Holiness.

JOHN PAUL looks at MARCINKUS for a moment.

JOHN PAUL: I can try. (*He stands up.*) It has been a pleasure meeting you, Bishop. Your comments should help me understand the audit.

MARCINKUS: (*Standing.*) The audit?

BENELLI: His Holiness has asked Villot to conduct an audit of the Bank.

JOHN PAUL: (*Putting his arm around MARCINKUS and walking him to the door.*) Thank you again, Bishop. It has been a pleasure. (*JOHN PAUL stops and holds out his ring. As MARCINKUS kisses it.*) Hopefully we will be able to get you home soon.

MARCINKUS looks at BENELLI and leaves.

BENELLI: Have you come to a decision?

JOHN PAUL: First Villot's report.

BENELLI: You have my report.

JOHN PAUL: Marcinkus might think you lack a little objectivity.

BENELLI: You talk about change. So far, all that has changed are ceremonies and symbols.

JOHN PAUL: I will change more than ceremonies.

BENELLI: And Villot and Felici?

JOHN PAUL: They will come around.

BENELLI: As long as they are here nothing will change.

JOHN PAUL: Are you so certain? These men are priests. They are men of God.

BENELLI: Once they were priests.

JOHN PAUL: Then I will remind them. They are my responsibility too, just like the poor and the weak.

BENELLI: They won't listen.

JOHN PAUL: Then I will pray for them.

BENELLI: Marcinkus was right. You can't run the Church with Hail Marys.

JOHN PAUL: Are you sure?

BENELLI: Then you don't need me.

JOHN PAUL: (*Simply.*) I need you.

BENELLI: I can't compete with the Holy Spirit. And I can't help you if you wish to save Villot and Felici's souls. (*Softly.*) Remove them.

JOHN PAUL: No.

BENELLI: Then I am going back to Florence.

JOHN PAUL: (*Pause.*) Perhaps that's best. No one should have to stay in Rome too long.

BENELLI: I wish I had your faith.

JOHN PAUL: All men have doubts at times, even Popes.

BENELLI: I have more than doubts.

JOHN PAUL is wearing a gold cross hanging from a gold chain around his neck. He takes the chain and cross off and looks at them.

JOHN PAUL: This was Pope Paul's, he gave it to me when he made me a cardinal. It had belonged to Pope John. (*He looks at BENELLI.*) I sold it when I was in Venice to raise money for charity when we lost the Catholic Bank. My people bought it back and gave it to me. (*He places the chain and cross around BENELLI's neck. BENELLI holds the cross in his hand and stares at it.*) Keep it.

BENELLI: Faith isn't regained through a cross.

JOHN PAUL: It is through other's belief. Think of the men who have worn it.

BENELLI: Felici, Villot, Baggio, they will all stop you.

JOHN PAUL: Only if God lets them.

BENELLI: (*Stares at JOHN PAUL for a moment.*) Perhaps it was the Holy Spirit at work in the conclave and not Cardinal Benelli.

JOHN PAUL: When you made me Pope, did you expect me to appoint you Secretary of State?

BENELLI: I expected you to do what you thought best for the Church. (*Pause.*) Do you forgive me?

JOHN PAUL: (*He blesses BENELLI.*) Go in peace, Cardinal Benelli. God forgives you.

The lights come up on the CONFESSOR. BENELLI joins him.

CONFESSOR: You walked away from power.

BENELLI: He would have made me Secretary of State if I had asked. I was too proud to ask.

CONFESSOR: Not many cardinals could have walked away from becoming Secretary of State.

BENELLI: In the end, I knew he would have to come to me. I loved him. But I wanted him to have to ask. So...I left him in Rome, surrounded by enemies, alone.

LORENZI: (*Enters.*) Do you need anything, Holy Father?

JOHN PAUL: No, I am going for a walk in the gardens. When Cardinal Villot and Cardinal Felici arrive tell them to meet me there.

LORENZI: They won't be happy about your going out alone.

JOHN PAUL: (*Pause. More to himself.*) A pope is always alone.

The POPE moves down stage. He encounters a gardener on his knees working.

THOMAS: Your Holiness...

JOHN PAUL: It is a beautiful garden. It reminds me of my old garden in the Dolomites.

THOMAS: Thank you, Your Holiness. (*He stands up and takes his hat off.*)

JOHN PAUL: What is your name?

THOMAS: Thomas.

JOHN PAUL: What does religion mean to you, Thomas?

THOMAS: Mass on Sundays.

JOHN PAUL: Anything else?

THOMAS: Things I can't do.

JOHN PAUL: (*JOHN PAUL crouches down.*) These flowers, Thomas, you take care of them.

THOMAS: (*Crouching down too.*) Yes, Holy Father.

JOHN PAUL: You water them, pull out the weeds, spray for insects.

THOMAS: Of course.

JOHN PAUL: Do you think they know it? (*Pause.*) God cares for you whether you know it or not. (*JOHN PAUL stands and gestures with his hand.*) What do you think of all this...the Vatican?

THOMAS: (*Stands and looks around.*) A palace your Holiness.

JOHN PAUL: A palace?

THOMAS: (*Now uncertain.*) A palace...for the Pope...for you to live in.

JOHN PAUL: (*Looking around.*) It does look like a palace...but it is a church.

THOMAS: It has guards Your Holiness, a church doesn't have guards.

JOHN PAUL: You are right... Do you think this is where the Pope should live? (*Silence.*) Where should the Bishop of Rome live?

THOMAS: (*Confused.*) ...With his people.

JOHN PAUL: Yes, with his people. (*VILLOT and FELICI enter. JOHN PAUL sees them.*) Thank you Thomas.

JOHN PAUL steps forward to meet VILLOT and FELICI. THOMAS waits for a moment and then exits.

VILLOT: You shouldn't talk to people like that.

JOHN PAUL looks inquisitively at VILLOT.

(*Defensively.*) Popes don't speak to gardeners.

JOHN PAUL: My father was a bricklayer.

VILLOT: Yes. (*Pause as he digests this unpleasant fact.*)

JOHN PAUL: It is time for me to visit Rome. I want to see every section, on foot.

VILLOT: Impossible.

JOHN PAUL: That word again.

FELICI: Thousands of people would flock to see you. The city would come to a halt.

JOHN PAUL: (*Thinking.*) Rome has hospitals?

VILLOT: Of course.

JOHN PAUL: It is the duty of a pastor to visit the sick and, as Bishop of Rome, to visit my churches. You will organise visits to every hospital, every church, every orphanage… (*VILLOT starts to speak.*) And do not tell me it is impossible.

JOHN PAUL: (*Starts to leave and then stops.*) And another thing: the article in the Vatican press about birth control.

VILLOT: An excellent article.

JOHN PAUL: People who read the article will assume that the opinions in it are mine.

FELICI: The opinions in the article are consistent with the position of the Church.

JOHN PAUL: (*Becoming angry.*) They are not consistent with my position and you know it… (*Calmer.*) Before Paul's

58

encyclical I submitted a report recommending that some
form of artificial birth control be permitted in marriage.
Last week the Vatican press denied my report ever existed.

VILLOT: We have located every copy. They are now locked in
the Vatican archives.

JOHN PAUL: That denial was a lie.

FELICI: It is the function of the Curia to protect a Pope from
possible mistakes that he made earlier in his life.

JOHN PAUL: I will decide if there were mistakes, not the
Curia. I did not want to become Pope. The Cardinals in
their infinite wisdom elected me, and I foolishly accepted.
But now I am the Pope.

VILLOT: No Pope can function without the assistance of the
Curia.

JOHN PAUL: (*Coldly.*) It appears that no Pope can function
with its assistance. It is the function of the Pope to set
policy, to govern, not the Curia and not the Vatican press.

VILLOT: The press was merely following the policy set out by
Pope Paul.

JOHN PAUL: By attacking a newborn baby, a baby I had just
congratulated in a letter. (*Furious.*) My church will not make
war on babies.

FELICI: The article condemned artificial conception, not
the child.

JOHN PAUL: The article condemned both. (*Pause. Calmly
and icily.*) Cardinal Felici, last week you told me that the
Curia wanted me to restrain what it called my 'natural
exuberance'.

FELICI: It was merely a suggestion, Your Holiness.

JOHN PAUL: I want you to return the compliment on my behalf. Tell that little newspaper to restrain its views. Editors are not indispensable. (*Turns and exits.*)

VILLOT: I will bury him in enough paper and reports to keep him busy twenty-four hours a day. He won't have time to do anything else.

FELICI: He will find the time.

VILLOT: He will destroy everything Pope Paul did.

FELICI: He will destroy the Church.

VILLOT: We made him Pope.

FELICI: Benelli made him Pope.

VILLOT: As long as he is Pope we have to obey.

FELICI: Popes are like editors, neither is indispensable.

> *The lights go down on VILLOT and FELICI. The lights come up on JOHN PAUL in his office. He is working behind his desk. LORENZI is stacking reports on a table. It is night and his desk light is on.*

CONFESSOR: He was strong, I did not realise how strong.

BENELLI: Truth carries its own strength.

CONFESSOR: He was a good man, but he was wrong.

BENELLI: He was the Pope, how could he be wrong?

CONFESSOR: (*Nodding grudgingly.*) He was the Pope.

LORENZI: Holy Father, it's very late. You have to get some sleep.

JOHN PAUL: I will soon.

JOHN PAUL is clearly exhausted. LORENZI pauses for a moment as he stacks another report.

LORENZI: Monsignor Magee says nothing was decided during Pope Paul's last year. (*JOHN PAUL continues to work.*) You can't solve a year's problems in just a few days.

JOHN PAUL: Some things can't wait any longer. I have to try.

LORENZI: Magee says Villot always gave Pope Paul summaries to read, not the full reports.

JOHN PAUL: (*Stops and looks at LORENZI.*) Summaries?

LORENZI: Magee should know.

JOHN PAUL: Yes, he should. Goodnight, Diego.

LORENZI leaves. JOHN PAUL sits thinking for a moment. He now realises what VILLOT is up to. He then picks up a bottle of pills on his desk, takes one and swallows it using a cup of coffee. He stands up, walks to an open window and breathes the air deeply. He then walks back to his desk, picks up the phone and places a call. He waits while the phone at the other end rings.

Cardinal Benelli, please… Yes, I know it's late… Yes, I know… Tell him it's the Pope…

The lights on JOHN PAUL go down as BENELLI talks.

BENELLI: He called me in Florence. His voice was quiet, calm. I could feel his resolve.

CONFESSOR: What did he say?

BENELLI: (*Smiling.*) That the truth is as hard to find in the Vatican as a good cup of coffee. He asked me to come back to Rome, to come back as Secretary of State. He was going to remove them all, Villot, Marcinkus, Baggio. He said it was time to send people home.

CONFESSOR: That was his right.

BENELLI: These were not ordinary priests, they were used to power.

CONFESSOR: He was the Pope, they had to obey.

BENELLI: As long as he lived, they had to obey. I warned him. I asked him to wait. To wait for me. (*Suddenly in pain, BENELLI bends over.*)

CONFESSOR: Are you alright?

BENELLI: (*Straightens. In an ill voice.*) Yes.

CONFESSOR: (*Concerned for the first time.*) You need to go to a hospital.

BENELLI: (*Regaining his breath.*) Do you fear death?

CONFESSOR: No.

BENELLI: (*Stares at him.*) I do. And the closer it comes, the more I am afraid.

CONFESSOR: (*Compassionately.*) Because you have lost God.

BENELLI: No. Because I might find him.

The lights go down.

Act Two

A light comes up on JOHN PAUL. He is at his desk working. He is also soaking his feet in a bowl of water. SISTER VINCENZA enters carrying a tray with a cup of coffee.

VINCENZA: Did you remember to take your pill last night?

JOHN PAUL: (*Looking up from his papers.*) Yes, Sister.

VINCENZA: The doctor says it will give you more energy.

JOHN PAUL: It will not make these papers disappear any faster.

VINCENZA: Would you like another cup of coffee?

JOHN PAUL: Thank you, the coffee is much better this morning.

VINCENZA: I bought a proper coffee-maker yesterday.

JOHN PAUL: (*Smiling.*) Perhaps the Vatican can change.

VINCENZA: How are your feet this morning?

JOHN PAUL: Better.

VINCENZA walks around the desk. JOHN PAUL takes his feet out of the bowl. VINCENZA takes a towel off the desk and kneels to dry JOHN PAUL's feet.

Sister, please, I can do that. (*She ignores him and starts drying his feet.*)

VINCENZA: Nonsense, Father, my old mother superior always said a nun's way to heaven is on her knees, praying or scrubbing.

JOHN PAUL: I am sure she didn't include drying feet. (*VINCENZA stands up.*) Thank you.

VINCENZA: (*Looking at a tray on the desk.*) You ate all your candies last night.

JOHN PAUL: (*Guilty.*) Yes Sister.

VINCENZA: Too many aren't good for you.

JOHN PAUL: I know Sister. (*LORENZI enters.*)

LORENZI: Cardinal Baggio is here for his meeting, Your Holiness.

JOHN PAUL: Just a minute, then send him in. Please let me know when Cardinal Villot is here. Can you take this with you, Diego?

LORENZI, carrying the bowl and towel, exits. JOHN PAUL starts putting on his sandals.

VINCENZA: Perhaps a few more candies for tonight.

JOHN PAUL: Thank you, Sister.

VINCENZA picks up the sweet plate and leaves. CARDINAL BAGGIO enters. He does not initially see the POPE, who is bent over behind his desk adjusting his sandals.

BAGGIO: Your Holiness. (*Looking around.*) Your Holiness. (*JOHN PAUL sits up.*)

JOHN PAUL: Good morning. (*Stands up.*) Thank you for coming. Overseeing all of the bishops must keep you very busy.

BAGGIO: It does, Holy Father. It's strange how few people appreciate that.

JOHN PAUL: How long have you been prefect?

BAGGIO: Seven years.

JOHN PAUL: And at the Vatican?

BAGGIO: Most of my career in the Church, almost thirty years.

JOHN PAUL: That is a long time to be away from parish work.

BAGGIO: I still say Mass every day, privately.

JOHN PAUL: (*Smiling.*) That isn't the same. Tell me about next month's South American conference.

BAGGIO: (*Pleased that the subject has changed.*) I have been planning it for over two years. It is going to be the first of this size in Latin America in decades.

JOHN PAUL: I understand Cardinal Lorscheider is working on the conference with you.

BAGGIO: (*Reluctantly.*) Yes.

JOHN PAUL: Cardinal Lorscheider and I have talked a great deal about the widespread poverty, the oppressive governments. He is strongly of the view that something has to be done to help these people.

BAGGIO: The Church has no place in politics. Right now, priests and nuns are fighting along with revolutionaries in Argentina and Colombia to overthrow legitimate governments.

JOHN PAUL: Can fascism ever be legitimate? Thousands of people have simply disappeared in Argentina. These governments are killing priests and nuns when they speak out.

BAGGIO: The business of the Church is religion.

JOHN PAUL: The business of the Church is men's souls. But it is hard to talk to a man about his soul when his children are starving. I will condemn any government that seeks to exploit its people.

BAGGIO: The Church cannot support violence.

JOHN PAUL: The Church cannot support oppression. I will go to South America.

BAGGIO: If you speak out you will destroy the Church in Latin America. The governments will turn on us.

JOHN PAUL: If the Pope does not speak out, who will? (*Silence.*) You realise that the diocese of Venice is vacant.

BAGGIO: (*Uncertain.*) Yes.

JOHN PAUL: The people of Venice are very dear to me. They need a cardinal to nourish and care for them. I want you to be that cardinal.

BAGGIO: (*Shocked.*) Me.

JOHN PAUL: Yes.

BAGGIO: But there is so much that I still have to do in Rome...my work...the bishops throughout the world...

JOHN PAUL: I want you to take care of Venice.

BAGGIO: (*Getting upset.*) You can't mean it.

JOHN PAUL: I do.

BAGGIO: (*Calmer.*) Thank you, but I must decline.

JOHN PAUL: You decline?

BAGGIO: I am needed here in Rome.

JOHN PAUL: I think it is my job to decide where my cardinals are needed. I want you to go to Venice.

BAGGIO: No.

JOHN PAUL: Cardinal Baggio, the matter is not open to debate.

BAGGIO: I am not leaving Rome.

JOHN PAUL: (*Pause.*) And your oath of obedience?

BAGGIO: I am a cardinal, a prince of the Church.

JOHN PAUL: I am the Pope.

BAGGIO: Your Holiness has much to learn.

JOHN PAUL: I am learning. I am not asking you to go to Venice, it is an order.

BAGGIO: (*Losing his temper.*) Not for me.

JOHN PAUL: (*Calm.*) You would defy the Pope?

BAGGIO: It takes more than new robes to make a Pope. It takes more than patting children on the head and telling funny stories. Thirty days ago you were a nobody in a backwater diocese preaching to empty churches and now you think you can rule the Roman Catholic Church. I am staying in Rome.

JOHN PAUL: Maybe I'm not much of a Pope, but you are going to Venice.

BAGGIO: (*Yelling.*) I'd sooner go to hell. (*LORENZI enters the room.*)

JOHN PAUL: (*Softly.*) I believe that can be arranged.

LORENZI: Your Holiness, Cardinal Villot is here. (*BAGGIO turns abruptly and storms out.*)

JOHN PAUL: Why would any priest want to be Pope?

LORENZI: Holy Father?

JOHN PAUL: Send Cardinal Villot in.

LORENZI exits. JOHN PAUL sits wearily at his desk. VILLOT enters.

Thank you for waiting. Would you like some coffee? (*He hesitates.*) Sister Vincenza's improved coffee.

VILLOT: Thank you, yes. (*JOHN PAUL pours each of them a cup.*) Cardinal Baggio looked upset.

JOHN PAUL: Yes. Tell me, is it usual for a cardinal to refuse to obey the Pope?

VILLOT: I don't understand.

JOHN PAUL: I just told Cardinal Baggio that I wanted him to replace me in Venice. He said no.

VILLOT: He said no?!

JOHN PAUL: Yes.

VILLOT: You agreed to reconsider?

JOHN PAUL: I want you to arrange for Cardinal Baggio's transfer.

VILLOT: If Your Holiness insists.

JOHN PAUL: I do. Please remind him that I did not want to come to Rome. Sometimes we have to sacrifice for the good of the Church.

VILLOT: I do not believe that Cardinal Baggio considers becoming Pope a sacrifice, but I will remind him.

JOHN PAUL: I've read your report on the Vatican Bank. I've also read Cardinal Benelli's report.

VILLOT: Benelli submitted a report?

JOHN PAUL: I have decided to remove Bishop Marcinkus.

VILLOT: When?

JOHN PAUL: Tomorrow.

VILLOT: Do you have another job for him in the Vatican?

JOHN PAUL: No, he is to be transferred to Chicago.

VILLOT: As Your Holiness wishes. (*Pause.*)

JOHN PAUL: How long have you been Secretary of State?

VILLOT: Ten years.

JOHN PAUL: It is a demanding job.

VILLOT: I have done my best.

JOHN PAUL: I know. You have earned the right to rest.

VILLOT: (*Pause.*) Does Your Holiness want me to retire?

JOHN PAUL: Yes.

VILLOT: (*There is a long pause.*) Cardinal Casaroli is a
good man.

JOHN PAUL: A brilliant diplomat…but he is too willing to
compromise with the communists.

VILLOT: Sometimes compromise is necessary.

JOHN PAUL: Sometimes, but not with communists.

VILLOT: Who is to be my replacement?

JOHN PAUL: Cardinal Benelli. (*There is a long pause.*)

VILLOT: You are the Pope.

JOHN PAUL: What do you think?

VILLOT: Your way is not Pope Paul's way.

JOHN PAUL: (*Wearily.*) I am not Pope Paul.

VILLOT: I fear for the Church.

JOHN PAUL: Why?

VILLOT: Because you are wrong.

JOHN PAUL: How am I wrong?

VILLOT: Everything about you is wrong.

JOHN PAUL: I am what I am. (*Pause.*)

VILLOT: Yes.

> *VILLOT exits. The phone rings. It is answered offstage. MAGEE enters.*

MAGEE: Your Holiness, it is Cardinal Suenens.

JOHN PAUL: I'll take it. (*MAGEE leaves and JOHN PAUL picks up the phone on his desk.*) Cardinal Suenens, how are you? I'm glad you called. It has not been a very good day. (*JOHN PAUL sits down.*) Yes, I would like to tell you about it.

As the lights go down on JOHN PAUL, they come up on BENELLI and the CONFESSOR.

BENELLI: Villot, Felici, Baggio, Marcinkus and always, somewhere, his friend Roberto Calvi. Does God will such things?

CONFESSOR: His plans are eternal.

BENELLI: Nothing is eternal, except greed and ambition and death.

CONFESSOR: God's love is eternal.

BENELLI: Then so is pain.

The lights come up on the Pope's study. It is later the same day and the light on the desk is on because it is dark out. An open bottle of pills, a basket of candies and a cup of coffee can be seen on the desk. MAGEE is in the room. JOHN PAUL enters.

MAGEE: (*Startled.*) Your Holiness.

JOHN PAUL: (*Smiling.*) Are you looking for something?

MAGEE: Yes…the book on the history of the papacy.

JOHN PAUL: That's over here.

JOHN PAUL walks over to a bookshelf and takes out a book. He opens the book and leafs through it for a moment.

You would have thought that God would have been kinder to those he chose. (*JOHN PAUL hands the book to MAGEE.*) How did Pope Paul feel as he neared the end of his reign?

MAGEE: That he had failed God.

JOHN PAUL: I can understand that.

MAGEE: Can I get you anything?

JOHN PAUL: (*Looking at his desk.*) A machine to do paperwork. (*Smiles.*) No, goodnight.

MAGEE: Goodnight, Holy Father.

MAGEE exits. JOHN PAUL takes a pill from the bottle on his desk, and using the cup of coffee swallows it. He then picks up a number of papers on the desk. As he picks up the papers, he notices that the tray of candies is full again. He smiles and takes a candy and eats it. He starts to leave, stops and comes back. BENELLI reacts. JOHN PAUL picks up the tray of candies. BENELLI watches. JOHN PAUL exits with the tray and the papers.

BENELLI: Villot called me the next morning, his voice was flat, without emotion. He read me the statement he was giving to the Vatican Radio. 'At five thirty in the morning of September the twenty-ninth, nineteen seventy-eight,

71

Monsignor Magee found the Pope dead in his bed. He was sitting up, with the light on reading 'The Imitation of the Life of Christ'. Death was due to a heart attack.' (*No longer quoting from the broadcast.*) He died on the thirty-third day of his reign. He was the first Pope in a century to die alone.

CONFESSOR: It was an act of God. You didn't kill him. You committed no sin.

BENELLI: Isn't pride a sin? Isn't anger a sin? Isn't desire for vengeance a sin? Isn't loss of faith a sin? I made him Pope and I abandoned him.

CONFESSOR: It was the will of God.

BENELLI: Was it? Was it so?

CONFESSOR: It's late. I have to leave.

BENELLI: Not until the end.

CONFESSOR: He is dead. That is the end. (*The CONFESSOR starts to leave.*)

BENELLI: When has the Church believed death is the end? (*The CONFESSOR stops.*) And so I went to Rome. Not as I had expected, as Secretary of State, but I went. I went to see Luciani. The Church had lost its soul...

The lights come up on the Pope's study. Everything has been removed except the books. BENELLI turns and walks into the study. He walks to the door of the Pope's bedroom. The Pope's body may be visible through the door. VINCENZA enters.

VINCENZA: May I see him?

BENELLI nods and turns away from the door. She goes to the door of JOHN PAUL's bedroom.

He looked so peaceful when I found him.

BENELLI: (*Curious.*) You found him?

VINCENZA: (*Emotional.*) He was sitting up in bed, his glasses were still on, his head was slightly to one side, his papers were in his lap.

BENELLI: His papers?

VINCENZA: Yes.

BENELLI: What papers?

VINCENZA: Lists of names. (*Looking at the body.*) He told me he was sending people home.

BENELLI: Villot said he was reading the 'Imitation of the Life of Christ'.

VINCENZA: No, he had his papers.

BENELLI: (*Looking around.*) Where are his things?

VINCENZA: Cardinal Villot had everything taken away… everything except his books.

BENELLI: (*Looking at the one book that is still on JOHN PAUL's desk.*) Was he reading about the lives of the Popes before he went to bed?

VINCENZA: No, that was Monsignor Magee.

BENELLI: (*Thinking about other things as he opens the book.*) I wonder why?

VINCENZA: I asked him last night. He said he wanted to know if Father Albino's reign was still the shortest of any Pope.

BENELLI: Last night, not this morning?

VINCENZA: Last night. (*Pause.*) May I go in to him?

BENELLI: Of course... Sister, did the Pope complain about any physical problem yesterday...chest pains, shortness of breath?

VINCENZA: No.

VINCENZA enters the bedroom and, if JOHN PAUL's body can be seen, kneels at the side of the bed. BENELLI picks up the book on the papacy from the desk. He walks to the doorway to the bedroom holding the book. He stares at the body of JOHN PAUL, then looks down at the book.

BENELLI: (*To LUCIANI.*) You were wrong about the Holy Spirit and I was wrong about Man. (*He approaches SISTER VINCENZA.*) Pray for us both, Sister...and pray for the Church.

A number of cardinals enter including FELICI, VILLOT, GANTIN, BAGGIO, OTTAVIANI, and one or two others. BENELLI moves to the CONFESSOR. The light on VINCENZA and JOHN PAUL slowly dims.

VILLOT: It is now our responsibility to schedule the funeral and prepare for the conclave. We must...

SUENENS: What about the rumours?

VILLOT: What rumours?

SUENENS: That his body was not discovered at five thirty by Magee, but at four thirty by a nun.

GANTIN: And that he died reading secret papers.

VILLOT: I can't be responsible for rumours.

LORSCHEIDER: Responsible newspapers are carrying the story.

VILLOT: These are lies by people trying to discredit the Vatican.

BAGGIO: Probably the communists.

BENELLI: (*BENELLI has moved half way between the CONFESSOR and the others.*) Is Sister Vincenza a communist?

VILLOT: Vincenza is in Venice.

BENELLI: I spoke to her. (*To VILLOT.*) Before you sent her away. (*To the others.*) She discovered the Pope's body a little after four thirty. He was holding papers he had been working on all afternoon.

OTTAVIANI: Impossible… Villot what is going on?

VILLOT: (*Looking around.*) How could I say a nun discovered the Pope's body?

OTTAVIANI: (*Shocked.*) So you lied to the press?

VILLOT: Yes.

GANTIN: And the story about what he was reading, was that a lie?

VILLOT: (*Looking at BENELLI, then speaking reluctantly.*) Yes.

OTTAVIANI: How could you do this?

BAGGIO: If we tell the truth now it will only be worse.

BENELLI: You can't hide the truth.

BAGGIO: Why not?

BENELLI: I won't hide the truth.

LORSCHEIDER: The newspapers are already saying that he might have been murdered.

OTTAVIANI: (*Looking at VILLOT.*) You are a fool.

BAGGIO: We can issue a correction and say it was a mistake.

OTTAVIANI gives BAGGIO a look of disdain.

OTTAVIANI: (*To BAGGIO.*) You are the mistake.

BENELLI: (*Slight pause.*) We need an autopsy.

VILLOT: The body has been embalmed.

BENELLI: I sent the embalmers away.

VILLOT: I sent them back. The body was embalmed last night.

BENELLI: Last night!

BAGGIO: (*Loudly.*) There will not be an autopsy.

GANTIN: Why not?

BAGGIO: There is no precedent.

SUENENS: Cardinal Felici, you are the expert.

FELICI: I don't know.

OTTAVIANI: If we have lied about the time, about the papers, people will think we have lied about the cause of death.

FELICI: There will always be rumours.

OTTAVIANI: (*Heated.*) Rumours about murder?

VILLOT: (*Trying to switch topics.*) We need to set a date for his funeral.

BENELLI: (*Not playing that game.*) What happened to his things? His personal effects, his papers.

VILLOT: I had them removed. His watch, glasses, pictures, that sort of thing were sent to his family.

BENELLI: And his papers?

VILLOT: They were confidential. They were destroyed.

GANTIN: Why?

VILLOT: I am the Secretary of State. It was my decision.

BENELLI: What about his pills?

VILLOT: Pills?

BENELLI: His pills, the coffee he drank that night, the tray of candies he kept on his desk?

VILLOT: I gave instructions to remove everything.

BENELLI: They were thrown out?!

VILLOT: Yes.

BENELLI: Then we will do an autopsy.

FELICI: An autopsy is ugly.

BENELLI: So is the possibility of murder.

BAGGIO: (*Abruptly.*) There will not be an autopsy.

> *Everyone looks at BAGGIO because of the force of his comment.*

> (*Trying to come up with a reason.*) How will we look? How will the Church look? It will only confirm people's suspicions and they will never believe the results anyway.

OTTAVIANI: I agree with Benelli.

FELICI: (*Sarcastically.*) That the Pope was murdered?

OTTAVIANI: That we should have an autopsy to prove he wasn't.

FELICI: (*Trying to avoid an autopsy.*) What we need is an informal investigation to see if there is any need for an autopsy. A very quiet inquiry.

OTTAVIANI: Let's carve the poor bastard up, prove he wasn't murdered and be done with it.

VILLOT: I don't know…

FELICI: (*Interrupting.*) As head of the Supreme Court, I will conduct the investigation.

OTTAVIANI: No. As Senior Cardinal I will head the investigation.

FELICI: I will assist.

BENELLI: And so will I. We will need Lorenzi.

VILLOT: I sent him north. I don't think…

BENELLI: We will need to speak to him and Monsignor Magee.

VILLOT: Magee has left Rome and hasn't been seen since.

OTTAVIANI: Find him.

Lights go down on the cardinals. Lights come up on OTTAVIANI and FELICI who are sitting. DR RENATO BUZZONETTI is also seated. BENELLI and the CONFESSOR are illuminated.

Dr Buzzonetti, you are the director of the Vatican Health Service.

BUZZONETTI: That is correct Your Eminence.

OTTAVIANI: (*Smiling benignly at him.*) We would just like to ask you a few questions about the morning you examined the body.

FELICI: Everything that is said here is completely confidential. Even the fact that we've had this meeting.

BUZZONETTI: I understand.

OTTAVIANI: You determined the cause of death.

BUZZONETTI: An acute myocardial infarction...that is heart failure, Your Eminence.

OTTAVIANI: (*Nodding, and looking at a paper.*) And you estimated his death occurred at approximately eleven p.m.?

BUZZONETTI: Probably while His Holiness was still awake.

OTTAVIANI: Why do you say that?

BUZZONETTI: The state of rigor mortis of the body...also his glasses were still on and the light by his bed was on.

OTTAVIANI: (*Pause.*) I see...

FELICI: Was there any evidence of some other cause of death?

BUZZONETTI: Such as?

FELICI: Anything unusual?

BUZZONETTI: No.

OTTAVIANI: Did you see any evidence that the Pope had been murdered?

BUZZONETTI: (*Shocked.*) Of course not.

OTTAVIANI: No, of course not.

BENELLI: (*To the CONFESSOR.*) So simple, isn't it? (*BENELLI moves towards the others.*)

OTTAVIANI: (*He looks at FELICI.*) Thank you very much, doctor. (*BUZZONETTI starts to leave.*)

BENELLI: Before determining that the Pope died of a heart attack how often had you examined him?

BUZZONETTI: His doctor was Dr Da Ros in Venice. I had never examined him.

OTTAVIANI: Never?!

BUZZONETTI: Not until he died.

BENELLI: Have you ever spoken to Dr Da Ros?

BUZZONETTI: Last week. He told me the Pope was in excellent health.

OTTAVIANI: He's dead.

BUZZONETTI: Before his death, he was in excellent health.

BENELLI: Did you speak with Dr Da Ros after he died?

BUZZONETTI: No.

BENELLI: Did you ask anyone if he had any symptoms, chest pains, shortness of breath?

BUZZONETTI: (*Becoming uncomfortable.*) No... I assume that if someone had noticed anything...they would have told me.

OTTAVIANI: No one told you about any symptoms?

BUZZONETTI: That is correct.

BENELLI: Then doctor, what was the basis for your diagnosis?

BUZZONETTI: Of course, a confident diagnosis can only be made after an autopsy and pathological examination.

BENELLI: I am aware of that. What was the basis for your diagnosis?

BUZZONETTI: (*A pause.*) He died suddenly while reading in bed. His complexion was slightly pale. These facts are consistent with a heart attack.

BENELLI: I have spoken to a number of heart specialists. They tell me that when people die of a heart attack, they are not found sitting up in bed with their glasses on. There is usually a tightness in the chest, often accompanied by severe pain along the left side. The Pope would have reacted to the pain. He would have made some effort to get help, to stay alive.

BUZZONETTI: (*Reluctantly.*) Perhaps.

BENELLI: There were alarm buttons on either side of the Pope's bed, centimetres from his hands. Would a heart attack have prevented him from pushing one of the buttons?

BUZZONETTI: (*Reluctantly.*) Not usually.

BENELLI: If, somehow, it did, wouldn't there still be some evidence of an attempt to reach them? (*Pause.*) Did you see any evidence of such an effort?

BUZZONETTI: No.

BENELLI: So how can you say the Pope died of a heart attack?

BUZZONETTI: I... He was the Pope. It must have been a heart attack.

BENELLI: (*Pause.*) Did you look for any evidence of poison?

BUZZONETTI: (*Shocked.*) No. Who would want to murder the Pope?

OTTAVIANI: No one. Are you finished Cardinal Benelli?

BENELLI: Yes.

OTTAVIANI: You're excused doctor. (*BUZZONETTI is leaving.*) God help us if we're ever sick. (*To FELICI.*) Where did we get him?

FELICI: He is really very competent. He helped treat Pope Paul for years.

OTTAVIANI: It's a wonder he lived so long. Who's next?

BENELLI: Lorenzi.

OTTAVIANI: Has Villot found Monsignor Magee?

FELICI: Yes, he has.

BENELLI: (*To the CONFESSOR.*) We met with Father Lorenzi. He was nervous, very nervous. He kept insisting he had nothing to hide.

CONFESSOR: Had he?

BENELLI: When Buzzonetti examined the Pope's body, Lorenzi never mentioned any symptoms. Now there was a pain?

CONFESSOR: What pain?

BENELLI: He said that Luciani complained of a severe pain at seven forty-five that evening.

CONFESSOR: Why didn't he tell Buzzonetti?

BENELLI: He said he didn't connect the pain with Luciani's death.

CONFESSOR: How could he fail to connect the two?

BENELLI: Why didn't he call a doctor?

MAGEE has entered while the CONFESSOR and BENELLI were talking.

OTTAVIANI: Monsignor. I am glad that you were able to interrupt your travels and visit us.

MAGEE: I came as soon as I learned you were looking for me. (*MAGEE sits down.*)

OTTAVIANI: I would like to know what happened the day the Pope died.

MAGEE: When the body was discovered?

BENELLI: No, the day before, the day he died. Were you there all day?

MAGEE: I had been there the entire thirty-two days. I hadn't left the papal apartments once.

BENELLI: So you were there all day, the day he died?

MAGEE: I... I went out at two thirty and was back by four thirty. That was the first and only time.

BENELLI: What was the Pope's schedule that morning?

MAGEE: He had appointments with Cardinal Baggio and Cardinal Villot.

BENELLI: Do you know what they discussed at the meetings?

MAGEE: (*Pause.*) No...

BENELLI: After that?

MAGEE: The Pope worked on papers from the Secretary of State until lunch.

BENELLI: What did he do after lunch?

MAGEE: He took a short nap and went for a walk.

BENELLI: In the Vatican Gardens?

MAGEE: No, Cardinal Villot didn't approve. He would usually go to the roof of the papal apartments and walk there.

BENELLI: Alone?

MAGEE: Always.

BENELLI: And the day he died?

MAGEE: It was cold that day and there was a strong wind. So he walked in the salon next to the secretaries' room.

OTTAVIANI: Like a prisoner in his own apartments.

MAGEE: Then Cardinal Villot called. He wanted to see the Pope again that evening. I interrupted His Holiness. He seemed upset, but he agreed. A little later, I heard a harsh coughing sound. He told me he had a pain and asked for Sister Vincenza. I found her and returned to the salon. Eventually, the pain went away.

BENELLI: Where was this pain?

MAGEE: (*A pause.*) I don't know.

BENELLI: Where was Father Lorenzi?

MAGEE: He was out. He didn't come back until much later, about seven o'clock.

FELICI: Are you certain?

MAGEE: Absolutely.

OTTAVIANI: But he suffered another pain at about seven forty-five?

MAGEE: The only time he complained was at five thirty in the afternoon.

BENELLI: And Father Lorenzi wasn't there?

MAGEE: That is what I said.

BENELLI: Father Lorenzi says he was there from three thirty on and that the only time the Pope felt a pain was at seven forty-five in the evening.

MAGEE: He is mistaken.

BENELLI: But he was there at seven forty-five?

MAGEE: (*Hesitantly.*) Yes.

BENELLI: Did you call a doctor?

MAGEE: No…his Holiness told me not to.

OTTAVIANI: Did you call Cardinal Villot and tell him what happened?

MAGEE: No. (*Pause.*) He was coming anyway.

OTTAVIANI: When the Pope was in pain and his life possibly at risk, you called no one? (*MAGEE is silent.*)

FELICI: When did Villot arrive?

MAGEE: At six thirty. He met with the Holy Father until about twenty to eight. After the meeting Cardinal Villot left and the Holy Father joined us for dinner.

BENELLI: Did the Holy Father complain about another pain when he came out of the meeting?

MAGEE: No.

BENELLI: Did you hear any of his conversation with Cardinal Villot?

MAGEE: No.

BENELLI: Did anyone else join you for dinner?

MAGEE: (*Pause.*) Cardinal Felici and Cardinal Baggio.

BENELLI: (*Staring at FELICI.*) What was discussed?

FELICI: Generalities. Nothing specific.

MAGEE: After dinner Their Eminences left and so did Father Lorenzi.

BENELLI: You were alone with the Pope?

MAGEE: Yes. The Holy Father and I went into his study. He picked up some papers and went to bed.

BENELLI: Sister Vincenza says that you read a book on the papacy that night.

MAGEE: (*Pause.*) Yes.

BENELLI: She says you decided to see if his reign was the shortest of any Pope's.

MAGEE: There were a few shorter but...

OTTAVIANI: That night, the night he died. The night before his body was discovered? (*Silence.*)

BENELLI: Why did you leave Rome?

MAGEE: The morning after the Pope died I was walking in the street. I passed one of his valets that I had fired a few days before. He pointed at me and said, 'There goes the murderer.' I didn't know what to do. I... Cardinal Villot was too busy to see me, so I went to see Bishop Marcinkus.

BENELLI: Marcinkus!

MAGEE: I knew he would help. I told him that I had been accused of killing the Pope and needed to get away. He arranged for a ticket in twenty minutes and I left immediately.

OTTAVIANI: When the Pope's body was discovered did you tell Dr Buzzonetti that the Pope had been in pain the day before?

MAGEE: No.

OTTAVIANI: You are excused. (*MAGEE leaves.*) One of them is lying.

FELICI: Or mistaken.

OTTAVIANI: Either Lorenzi was there when the pain happened or he wasn't. The pain was either at five thirty or at seven forty-five. This was the day the Pope died. How can you confuse things like this? One of them has to be lying.

BENELLI: Or both.

OTTAVIANI: We will break for lunch. (*To BENELLI.*) Who is next?

BENELLI: Cardinal Villot.

OTTAVIANI: Villot!

BENELLI: Villot.

BENELLI moves across the stage and is joined by SUENENS and GANTIN. The lights go down on OTTAVIANI and FELICI. If desired, groups of cardinals, including OTTAVIANI and FELICI, can walk about the stage. They are preparing for the conclave.

SUENENS: When will you finish?

BENELLI: I don't know.

GANTIN: The funeral and the conclave can't be put off.

BENELLI: It may be necessary.

SUENENS: And what will we tell the world?

BENELLI: The truth.

SUENENS: Then let us pray that you finish today.

GANTIN: We need to prepare for the conclave. We need to decide who we want as the next Pope.

BENELLI: First, we need to bury the old one.

GANTIN: We will.

BENELLI: Did you read what Baggio said to the press when asked about John Paul's death?

GANTIN: No.

BENELLI: The Lord uses us, but does not need us. Now we will make another one.

GANTIN: Baggio could be the next Pope.

SUENENS: Or Felici.

BENELLI: No.

GANTIN: I once asked you if you would consider a higher office. I am asking again.

SUENENS: We want you to be the next Pope. (*Pause.*)

GANTIN: The Africans, the South Americans, most of the Europeans, they all want you.

BENELLI: I...will consider it.

GANTIN bows slightly and exits.

(*Vehemently.*) Luciani isn't even buried.

SUENENS: He's with God. We are not so fortunate.

BENELLI: You, like him, have so much faith.

SUENENS: Sometimes.

BENELLI: Sometimes I have doubts.

SUENENS: So do most men.

BENELLI: Most men are not thinking of becoming Pope...

SUENENS: We had Luciani. Perhaps now we need a Pope who knows what it is to grope his way to God.

BENELLI: What if I don't find him?

SUENENS: You found Luciani.

BENELLI: And left him to die.

SUENENS: God made him Pope and God let him die.

BENELLI: Why let a man like Luciani become Pope and then take him away in thirty-three days?

SUENENS: Why does He ever let evil triumph...? I don't know why.

BENELLI: Have you seen Luciani? Have you seen...his body? (*SUENENS shakes his head no.*) He seemed so small, so empty. God is supposed to be everywhere. I looked into Luciani's dead eyes. I did not see God. I felt his cold hand. I did not feel God. What if there is...nothing? What if it is not the hand of God acting?

SUENENS: We are God's instruments.

BENELLI: And Felici and Villot?

SUENENS: (*Grimly.*) We are all God's instruments.

BENELLI: I have spent my life watching priests who should be holy men struggle for power, as I have. I have risen, gained power, used it... I made Luciani Pope because I knew he was one man power could not change. He was a holy man. I am no Luciani.

SUENENS: Perhaps he was too perfect for this world.

BENELLI: Anyone but me.

SUENENS: There is no one else.

BENELLI: There are other cardinals.

SUENENS: Baggio, Villot, Felici? If you do not agree one of them will be the next Pope.

BENELLI: Absolute power...my hand rather than theirs...

BENELLI and SUENENS turn and walk together.

SUENENS: I spoke to Luciani the day he died. (*BENELLI stops and looks at SUENENS.*) He told me about his meeting with Baggio. He also told me about his meeting with Villot and his decision on Marcinkus.

BENELLI: What happened?

SUENENS: He was sending them home.

The lights switch to OTTAVIANI, VILLOT and FELICI

FELICI: Thank you for coming. I know how busy you are.

VILLOT: The funeral arrangements and the conclave.

As CARDINAL BENELLI joins them.

OTTAVIANI: Of course.

BENELLI: I located the valet Magee claims accused him of murder. He denies ever accusing him.

OTTAVIANI: (*To VILLOT.*) Cardinal Benelli has a few questions.

VILLOT: (*To BENELLI.*) Try to be brief.

BENELLI: We are here to discuss the death of a Pope.

VILLOT: All men die, even Popes.

BENELLI: It is one thing to die; it is another thing to be killed.

VILLOT: No one killed the Pope.

BENELLI: Tell me about Pope Paul.

VILLOT: What?

BENELLI: What did you think of him? (*VILLOT looks briefly at OTTAVIANI and FELICI.*)

VILLOT: He was a great Pope. He was trained in the discipline of the Curia. He was learned, a scholar, an intellectual, a man who cared deeply for the Church and who thought carefully before coming to decisions.

BENELLI: What was his greatest achievement?

VILLOT: His encyclical on birth control.

BENELLI: What do you want in the next Pope?

VILLOT: A greater Paul. A man to carry his work forward, a man of authority and discipline.

BENELLI: And compassion?

VILLOT: Compassion is for priests, not for Popes.

BENELLI: And not for Secretaries of State.

VILLOT: My function is to run the Church.

BENELLI: Yet you let Luciani change the investiture ceremony.

VILLOT: It was a ceremony a thousand years old. He changed it on a whim, as if it were just the organisation of a garden party.

BENELLI: And you let him.

VILLOT: He was the Pope.

BENELLI: And as long as he was the Pope you had to obey.

VILLOT: Yes.

BENELLI: Tell us about his feelings toward Paul's encyclical on birth control.

VILLOT: (*Pause.*) We would have convinced him.

BENELLI: Of what?

VILLOT: That Pope Paul was right.

BENELLI: How could you if you were no longer here?

VILLOT: What do you mean?

BENELLI: You were leaving Rome.

VILLOT: I had no intention of leaving Rome.

BENELLI: On September the twenty-eighth, the day the Pope died, he told you that he was removing you as Secretary of State.

VILLOT: How dare you say that?

BENELLI: I don't say it, Cardinal Suenens does.

OTTAVIANI: Suenens?

BENELLI: He spoke to John Paul right after the Pope's meeting with Cardinal Villot.

OTTAVIANI: And who was to replace Cardinal Villot?

BENELLI: I was. (*Back to VILLOT.*) Do you deny it?

VILLOT: (*Looks at OTTAVIANI and then FELICI.*) I don't deny it.

BENELLI: And later that evening you returned. You came to see the Pope one final time.

VILLOT: I saw the Pope frequently.

BENELLI: You had just been removed. You returned to try to get the Pope to change his mind.

VILLOT: He was going to destroy everything that Pope Paul accomplished.

BENELLI: And you failed.

VILLOT: He wouldn't listen.

BENELLI: And the papers were already drawn up. The papers removing you and others.

VILLOT: He had papers.

BENELLI: And that night he took them to bed with him.

VILLOT: He was going to remove the best people in the Curia.

BENELLI: He was the Pope and you had to obey.

VILLOT: I did not have to obey.

BENELLI: As long as he lived you had to obey. (*Pause.*) What happened that evening of September the twenty-eighth? Was it the coffee? Was it the candies he loved? Was it his bottle of pills?

VILLOT: There is no evidence he was poisoned.

BENELLI: You destroyed the evidence.

VILLOT: No Pope is more important than the Church. The Curia has defeated greater Popes than John Paul.

BENELLI: And how would you have stopped him?

VILLOT: I buried him in paper.

BENELLI: But he made decisions.

VILLOT: And we told him no.

BENELLI: Again and again you told him no.

VILLOT: Yes.

BENELLI: And day after day the piles of paper grew higher.

VILLOT: Yes.

BENELLI: For a year nothing had been decided. Now in one month you poured on his shoulders every problem you could find.

VILLOT: He was the Pope. He had to make the decisions.

BENELLI: And when he made them, you told him no.

VILLOT: He was wrong. (*BENELLI stares at him.*) I am the Secretary of State. It is my right to tell the Pope he is wrong.

BENELLI: It is the Pope's right to make the final decisions.

VILLOT: Error has no rights.

BENELLI: Are you saying the Pope was in error?

VILLOT: Every word. Every action.

BENELLI: Who are you to judge the Pope?

VILLOT: He wasn't a Pope. He was a country priest that you pushed into the papacy. He was your Pope, not ours.

BENELLI: And this country priest had ideas of his own. Ideas he was willing to fight for.

VILLOT: He would have destroyed the Church.

BENELLI: Who made you the final arbiter?

VILLOT: The Curia is the Church.

BENELLI: He would have changed the Curia.

VILLOT: I would have stopped him.

BENELLI: He removed you. There was only one way you could stop him.

VILLOT: I did not murder the Pope.

BENELLI: You drove him. You couldn't change him. So you isolated him and drove him.

VILLOT: (*Stands up.*) Yes, I drove him. I drove him day and night.

BENELLI: He was in error. He was wrong.

VILLOT: He was the error.

BENELLI: He would have destroyed the Church.

VILLOT: Yes.

BENELLI: He had to die.

VILLOT: Yes.

BENELLI: He had to die for the Church.

VILLOT: Yes, I drove him – I worked him – I drove him until his body – until he died. Yes… God help me…I killed the Pope. (*The room is silent.*)

BENELLI: (*Softly.*) We all killed him.

OTTAVIANI: Cardinal Villot… (*VILLOT looks up at OTTAVIANI.*) You are excused. (*VILLOT stands and exits.*) So that's that. God help him.

BENELLI: Who?

OTTAVIANI: Cardinal Villot… I think we are at an end.

BENELLI: No. We need to see Marcinkus, Baggio…

OTTAVIANI: Further investigation could take weeks.

BENELLI: There is another witness.

OTTAVIANI: Who?

BENELLI: Cardinal Felici.

OTTAVIANI: This investigation is concluded.

BENELLI: It will conclude when I am done.

OTTAVIANI: The press will announce to the world that the Church has put off the funeral of the last Pope and the election of the new Pope to investigate whether the last Pope was murdered by his cardinals and bishops. Are you mad?!

FELICI: (*To OTTAVIANI.*) Perhaps you might give me a few minutes with Cardinal Benelli?

OTTAVIANI: (*Reluctantly.*) Very well. (*OTTAVIANI leaves.*)

FELICI: It is over.

BENELLI: Not yet.

FELICI: John Paul died. It was God's will.

BENELLI: Maybe God made him Pope, but men killed him.

FELICI: No one murdered the Pope.

BENELLI: The autopsy will determine that.

FELICI: There will be no autopsy. Tomorrow the Pope is scheduled to be buried and tomorrow he will be buried.

BENELLI: I wonder what kind of God you pray to?

FELICI: I wonder if you have a God. (*Pause.*)

BENELLI: Villot didn't murder the Pope. He isn't hard enough. But others are. You would have killed Christ to save your Church.

FELICI: The death of Christ is not at issue.

BENELLI: The death of his Pope is.

FELICI: Which is more important, justice for one dead man
or the life of Christ's Church? Let us assume you are right.
Let us assume someone murdered the Pope. It might have
been someone outside of the Church…but let us assume
it was someone in the Church. Balance the harm your
investigation will cause the Church against the benefit of
punishing one man or even a group of men. In the end,
God will be their judge.

BENELLI: What God chooses to do is his business. Luciani's
death is mine.

FELICI: You will establish nothing without an autopsy and for
that you need a precedent.

BENELLI: There is precedent.

FELICI: (*Slowly nodding.*) Pius VIII…yes, you can force an
autopsy and the investigation. But what you really want
is Villot, Marcinkus, myself and others, out of Rome. You
will not accomplish that with an autopsy. The only way
you can is if you become the next Pope.

BENELLI: Then I will become Pope.

FELICI: The man who puts off the conclave and forces the
Church to announce an investigation to the world will
never become Pope.

BENELLI: So, it isn't about my love for Luciani. It isn't about
religion or the Church. It isn't about God…

FELICI: (*Interrupting.*) It is about power. Luciani was a saint.
Churches are not run by saints. They are run by men who
understand power. In five days we are going into conclave
to elect the next Pope. End the investigation now and you

97

could be that Pope. You could have the power to remake the Church.

OTTAVIANI enters.

OTTAVIANI: (*To BENELLI.*) Have you come to a decision?

FELICI: (*Looking at BENELLI.*) The investigation has concluded.

The lights go down on FELICI and OTTAVIANI. BENELLI moves across the stage and joins the CONFESSOR.

BENELLI: At the moment that mattered most, I chose wrong, and with my choice, somewhere there was a sigh. What could have been would never be. (*BENELLI stares at the CONFESSOR for a moment.*) That was my final sin.

CONFESSOR: You chose to be Pope, that isn't a sin.

BENELLI: I chose power.

CONFESSOR: Religion is power. The power to direct men's lives. The power to govern their souls.

BENELLI: I thought so once. But not now.

CONFESSOR: Then what is it?

BENELLI: I think it is about Man's relationship with God.

BENELLI starts to move away from the CONFESSOR, and the lights slowly go down on the CONFESSOR.

On October the fourth John Paul was buried, as scheduled. Over six hundred thousand people, four times as many as had come to see Paul, filed past his body as it lay in state, surrounded by all the pomp and ceremony that he had refused in life. In death the smile was finally gone. It was a cold, grey day, the day he was buried. It rained on and off. Still hundreds of thousands more came to say goodbye. A reporter said it best: it was as if a parish had lost its priest. Five days later the Cardinals of the Roman Catholic Church once more gathered together. Once more they went into conclave to elect the next successor to Peter, the next Pope. And I, Cardinal Benelli, a man without faith, had decided to become that Pope.

Lights come up on GANTIN and SUENENS. They are in conclave. BENELLI moves across the stage and joins them.

SUENENS: (*To BENELLI.*) You have sixty-five votes and it is only the third ballot. Siri is finished. His support has dropped to twelve votes.

BENELLI: His interview in the press destroyed his chances.

SUENENS: (*Laughing.*) He attacked John Paul – he insulted Villot – he abused the reporter. The real Siri came out.

GANTIN: Apparently he had an understanding with the reporter that the article would not be published until after the cardinals went into conclave and were isolated. (*Unhappy about the way things have happened. Speaking to BENELLI.*) There are rumours that you spoke to the reporter.

BENELLI: Siri broadcast a sanitised version. The reporter decided that released him from his promise.

GANTIN: You spoke to him?

BENELLI: He called me. It was the reporter's decision.

GANTIN: (*Still unhappy.*) I see.

BENELLI: Yes. (*They stare at each other for a moment.*)

GANTIN: And Siri's supporters have simply shifted to Felici.

BENELLI: Felici has always been the real threat.

SUENENS: He has thirty votes. Even with all the conservatives and Curia cardinals supporting him, that is about as far as he can go.

BENELLI: He only needs thirty-six votes to block another candidate.

SUENENS: He knows he can't win. He is already looking for a compromise candidate that he can control.

GANTIN: He and Villot have been talking to Cardinal Colombo.

SUENENS: (*To BENELLI.*) You need to talk to Colombo this evening.

BENELLI: I already have.

SUENENS: What did you tell him.

BENELLI: The truth. He is seventy-six years old and cannot fight Felici and the others.

SUENENS: Was he convinced?

BENELLI: I convinced him.

GANTIN: In my country there is a saying: if you feed like the jackal you become the jackal. How are we different from Felici?

SUENENS: (*Laughing.*) Because we're right, of course.

GANTIN: (*Shocked. To BENELLI.*) Your Eminence?

BENELLI: (*Pause.*) I don't know…but Felici is not becoming Pope.

The lights go down and simultaneously come up on the other side of the stage on FELICI, BAGGIO and VILLOT.

VILLOT: Colombo has withdrawn.

BAGGIO: Impossible. Yesterday he agreed to be a candidate.

VILLOT: Benelli spoke to him.

BAGGIO: Benelli!

VILLOT: He is going to be Pope.

FELICI: Not yet.

VILLOT: He is up to seventy votes. He only needs five more.

BAGGIO: First he destroyed Siri, now he has convinced Colombo not to run.

FELICI: We will find another Italian candidate.

BAGGIO: There aren't any other Italian cardinals that will be acceptable to the non-Italians.

FELICI: Then we will have to find a non-Italian.

VILLOT: The Pope has been Italian for five hundred years.

BAGGIO: Better a non-Italian than having to kiss Benelli's papal ring.

FELICI: What about Cardinal Wojtyla? He has nine votes.

BAGGIO: The Austrians and Germans are supporting him.

FELICI: I like his theology, conservative.

VILLOT: Perhaps too conservative.

BAGGIO: Now isn't the time to quibble over theology. Better a heretic than Benelli as Pope.

VILLOT: It will take time to put a coalition together. (*To FELICI.*) How long can you hold your support?

FELICI: Long enough.

BAGGIO: He only needs five votes.

FELICI: Most of my supporters are afraid of Benelli. The rest are afraid of me. I can hold them.

VILLOT: Where is the weakness in Benelli's support?

BAGGIO: Lorscheider. He is voting for Benelli but he would love to see a non-Italian Pope.

VILLOT: And Benelli respects him for risking his life by standing up to Brazil's military government.

FELICI: Then we will give him his non-Italian Pope.

The lights go down and simultaneously come up on BENELLI, SUENENS and GANTIN.

GANTIN: Felici is still holding his support together.

SUENENS: We only need five more votes.

BENELLI: One of the cardinals I tried to convince told me Felici had threatened him with the Vatican archives.

GANTIN: The archives?

BENELLI: Felici is one of the few people with access to the archives. If a cardinal has even thought of sinning it's listed there. Felici always has understood the power of moral persuasion.

SUENENS: We can still win.

BENELLI: Five votes.

LORSCHEIDER enters.

LORSCHEIDER: (*To BENELLI.*) Your Eminence – forgive me. The conclave is deadlocked.

BENELLI: I know.

LORSCHEIDER: Something needs to be done.

BENELLI: What about the nine votes for Wojtyla?

LORSCHEIDER: Cardinal Ratzinger is keeping the Germans and Austrians behind him. I can't move them. And Felici is still holding the conservatives together.

SUENENS: It's only five votes.

LORSCHEIDER: You can't get them.

BENELLI: What do you suggest?

LORSCHEIDER: We need to find a compromise. I met with Felici this morning. He has proposed Wojtyla.

GANTIN: A Polish Pope!

SUENENS: The thought must make Villot's teeth grind.

LORSCHEIDER: He has no connection with the Curia.

SUENENS: Then why would Felici suggest him?

LORSCHEIDER: I don't know. But we can't elect a Pope without some of Felici's or Wojtyla's votes.

BENELLI: Tell me about Wojtyla.

LORSCHEIDER: You know him.

BENELLI: Not well.

LORSCHEIDER: Nor do I. But I do know that he has stood up against the communists in Poland. He has urged his people to seek higher wages and better working conditions, to be politically active. That is exactly what we need in South America to deal with the dictatorships.

BENELLI: And what about implementing the decisions of the Second Vatican Council to open the Church up to new ideas and to have closer communication with other religions?

LORSCHEIDER: He says that he is committed to the Second Vatican Council.

BENELLI: You spoke to him?

LORSCHEIDER: Yes.

BENELLI: And you believe him?

LORSCHEIDER: Who knows what will happen to a man when he puts on the Fisherman's ring.

BENELLI: I knew with Luciani.

LORSCHEIDER: There is very little choice. Felici controls thirty votes and nine are firmly committed to Wojtyla. We need five of those votes. You will not accept Felici. He will not accept you. That leaves Wojtyla.

GANTIN: In the last conclave we left feeling that we had been inspired by the Holy Spirit.

BENELLI: Not in this conclave.

LORSCHEIDER: God has to work through the men he has available.

SUENENS: (*To BENELLI.*) There is no need to compromise. We can force Felici to stay here until he rots.

LORSCHEIDER: (*To BENELLI.*) You are the only Italian cardinal that I will vote for. If you want me to hold the South Americans, I will. If you want we will stay here until we all rot. But what will that do to the Church? What authority will the next Pope have if it is obvious that he was not the first or even second choice of the majority of cardinals? How will the world regard him?

BENELLI: You are asking me to walk away from the papacy.

LORSCHEIDER: It is your decision. I will do whatever you want.

BENELLI: Is there no other way?

LORSCHEIDER: No.

BENELLI looks at GANTIN who shakes his head and then looks down and away.

SUENENS: We can still win.

BENELLI: (*To LORSCHEIDER.*) Now I understand how you have faced down governments.

LORSCHEIDER: That was easy. I knew they were wrong.

BENELLI, thinking, touches the cross hanging from his neck – JOHN PAUL's gift. He then looks at SUENENS for a moment and then back to LORSCHEIDER.

BENELLI: Wojtyla will be the next Pope.

LORSCHEIDER walks over to BENELLI and takes his hand. Instead of shaking it, LORSCHEIDER kneels and kisses BENELLI's ring.

It isn't the papal ring.

LORSCHEIDER: It is to me. (*LORSCHEIDER and GANTIN leave.*)

SUENENS: Only five votes.

BENELLI: It would have cost the Church too much to get them.

SUENENS: You would have made a great Pope.

BENELLI: (*With a wry smile.*) I don't think I was meant to wear white.

The lights go down on BENELLI and SUENENS. Cardinals enter and line up across the back of the stage. They are dimly lit. Their faces cannot be seen. As the cardinals enter, VILLOT's voice can be heard from the darkness stage-right counting the ballots.

VILLOT: A vote for Cardinal Wojtyla, a vote for Cardinal Wojtyla... Cardinal Wojtyla... Cardinal Wojtyla. (*There is silence.*) The final tally is, one hundred and three votes for Caridnal Wojtyla and seven abstentions.

VILLOT steps towards the centre of the stage and is illuminated as he stops in front of one of the cardinals. The cardinals are still only dimly lit.

Do you accept your election as Supreme Pontiff?

VOICE: (*From out of the darkness. A pause.*) I accept.

VILLOT: By what name do you wish to be called?

CONFESSOR stepping into the light.

CONFESSOR: John Paul II. (*There is a pause then the lights go out.*)

When the lights come up, BENELLI and the CONFESSOR are in BENELLI's study in Florence. It is almost morning.

BENELLI: Why wouldn't you see me?

CONFESSOR: I knew you would make me reopen the investigation.

BENELLI: Why did you keep them all in Rome? Felici, Villot, Marcinkus...

CONFESSOR: Villot died six months later.

BENELLI: Why did you swear Magee to silence?

CONFESSOR: To protect the Church.

BENELLI: And what about Marcinkus? Last June his friend
Calvi was found hanging from a bridge in London with
a brick in each pocket. His Bank Ambrosiano collapsed.
One point two billion dollars disappeared through shell
companies whose stock was held in the name of Bishop
Marcinkus.

CONFESSOR: Marcinkus made an honest mistake.
The Church will pay what it should.

BENELLI: Pope John and the Second Vatican Council opened
the windows of the Church to the world. For four years I
have watched you close them, one by one.

CONFESSOR: I have told the world that for the Church,
morality is not a matter of convenience.

BENELLI: And Luciani's death, was that a matter of
convenience?

CONFESSOR: I will not listen to any more about Luciani.

BENELLI: You told Lorscheider that you would not permit
priests to be politically active in South America.

CONFESSOR: Christ was not a revolutionary.

BENELLI: He was the greatest revolutionary.

CONFESSOR: The business of the Church is God.

BENELLI: It is men searching for God... When you look in the
mirror, what do you see...infallibility?

CONFESSOR: I see the man God chose to be Pope. You
lack faith. Faith is the will to believe in something greater
than yourself. I can help you find that will. Forget this
confession. (*He points to the written confession.*) I will help
you find God.

BENELLI: (*Stares at the Pope, wanting to accept.*) Faith can't simply be given, not even by a Pope... I have lived here for four years knowing all the while I have failed. I failed the Church, I failed myself. I failed Luciani.

CONFESSOR: Forget Luciani.

BENELLI: I can't. I watched him during his thirty-three days as Pope and after he died... I sat in the conclave five votes away from the Papacy and, when I spoke to Lorscheider and decided to walk away, it was as if...I brushed the hand of God... (*He looks at the CONFESSOR and regains his strength and sense of purpose.*) You cannot build the Church on edicts and lies.

CONFESSOR: What would you build it on?

BENELLI: Compassion and the truth.

CONFESSOR: We live in a world that takes advantage of compassion and twists the truth.

BENELLI: What have you demanded of the world?

CONFESSOR: That it live in accordance with Christ's word.

BENELLI: How can you demand less of the Church?

CONFESSOR: You don't know that Luciani was murdered.

BENELLI: One way or another men defied him and then killed him, and you have done nothing about it.

CONFESSOR: I will hear no more about Luciani.

BENELLI: You will hear what I tell you.

CONFESSOR: I am the Pope.

BENELLI: I have made Popes. I made you, Pope... I have committed sins, sins of pride and the desire for power. What have you committed by averting your eyes?

CONFESSOR: The Church is more than the Vatican. It is greater than the men who run her. It is greater than any Pope. And there are things I must do as Pope to protect the Church... But I am also a man.

The CONFESSOR walks over to BENELLI until they are very close and stares at him for a moment. Then the CONFESSOR slowly sinks to his knees.

Will you grant me absolution?

BENELLI: (*BENELLI stares at him for a moment. Then he slowly raises his right hand.*) Do you acknowledge before God that you are sorry for your sins and do you promise to sin no more?

There is a pause while BENELLI holds up his hand ready to grant absolution. The CONFESSOR finally looks up at him.

CONFESSOR: No. What I have done, I have done for my Church. (*BENELLI lowers his hand.*)

BENELLI: Then I cannot grant you absolution.

The CONFESSOR stands. BENELLI walks to the table and picks up his confession.

I will publish my confession.

CONFESSOR: Every enemy will use it against us.

BENELLI: I will prove to the Church that it is great enough to be wrong.

CONFESSOR: I order you not to publish.

BENELLI: I am dying. Only God can order me now.

CONFESSOR: I am willing to risk the loss of my immortal soul for the Church. What are you willing to risk?

BENELLI: That is between me and God.

The two men stand staring at each other.

CONFESSOR: Then I will leave you to God. (*The CONFESSOR starts to leave and then stops.*) And may God have mercy on your soul. (*The CONFESSOR leaves.*)

BENELLI stands for a moment, then turns and looks at the confession. He picks it up and stands holding it. With a slight smile, remembering his words.

BENELLI: ...as if I brushed the hand of God...

A long pause as he reaches out for God. Finally...

It isn't about Luciani, it isn't about the Church, it *is* about faith.

He reaches a decision. He takes a box of matches from the table.

So be it.

He lights the confession, holds it, then drops it into a metal waste basket, looking up as it burns.

Almighty God, into your hands I deliver my spirit. (*He sinks slowly into the chair. He is dying.*) To your grace and wisdom I leave your Church.

As the lights go down, BENELLI slumps slowly back in his chair. He looks up and then his head sags to one side. Now he is illuminated only by the burning confession. The lights finally fade as the confession turns to ashes.

Blackout.

Postscript

On October 26, 1982, Cardinal Giovanni Benelli died. The hospital announced that his death was the result of a heart infarction – due to complications arising from his refusal to go to the hospital on a timely basis for treatment. The Vatican issued an immediate denial.

On June 30, 1984, the Vatican paid 250 million dollars to settle claims brought against it arising out of the collapse of Bank Ambrosiano. The Italian government issued an arrest warrant for Bishop Marcinkus. The arrest never took place as he remained for years in the sanctuary of the Vatican. Bishop Marcinkus was promoted to Archbishop and kept on as the head of the Vatican Bank.

WWW.OBERONBOOKS.COM

Follow us on www.twitter.com/@oberonbooks
& www.facebook.com/OberonBooksLondon

9 781840 027792